Zen Light

Unconventional Commentaries on the *Denkoroku*

By Stefano Mui Barragato, Sensei

Zen Light

Unconventional Commentaries on the *Denkoroku*

By Stefano Mui Barragato, Sensei

Charles E. Tuttle Co., Inc.
Boston • Rutland, Vermont • Tokyo

First published in 1997 by Tuttle Publishing, an imprint of Periplus Editions (HK) Ltd., with editorial offices at 153 Milk Street, Boston, Massachusetts 02109.

Copyright © 1997 Stefano Barragato

All rights reserved. No part of this publication may be reproduced or utilized in any form or by any means, electronic or mechanical, including photocopying, recording, or by any information storage and retrieval system, without prior written permission from Tuttle Publishing.

The use of the koans as well as text on pages 155 and 174 is reproduced from *The Record of Transmitting the Light: Zen Master Keizan's Denkoroku*. Translated by Francis H. Cook, © 1991, Zen Center of Los Angeles. Reproduced by permission of the Zen Center of Los Angeles. All rights reserved.

Library of Congress Cataloging–in–Publication Data

Barragato, Stefano, 1930–
    Zen light : unconventional commentaries on the Denkoroku / Stefano Barragato. —1st ed.
      p. cm.
    ISBN 0-8048-3106-8
    1. Keizan, 1268–1325. Denkoroku. 2. Sotoshu. 3. Priests, Zen-–Biography. I. Keizan, 1268–1325. Denkoroku. II. Title.
BQ9449.S544D463 1997
294.3'927—dc21   97–5244
                                                                               CIP

Distributed by

Charles E. Tuttle Co., Inc.	Tuttle Shokai Ltd.
RR1 Box 231-5	1-21-13, Seki
North Clarendon, VT	Tama-ku, Kawasaki-shi
05759	Kanagawa-ken, 214
tel: (800) 526-2778	Japan
fax: (800) FAX-TUTL	tel: (044) 833-0225
	fax: (044) 822-0413

Berkeley Books Pte. Ltd.
5 Little Road #08-01
Singapore 536983
tel: (65) 280-3320
fax: (65) 280-6290

First Edition
1 3 5 7 9 10 8 6 4 2   05 04 03 02 01 00   99 98 97

Cover design by Jill Winitzer
Design by Fran Kay

Printed in the United States of America

. . . coming from the heart, may it again reach the heart.

•

—Ludwig van Beethoven

To Margaret, my wife, friend, companion, goad, and fellow recluse.

To students of the White Cliff and Dragon Gate Sanghas, who have helped me with this book by listening to me read it to them in place of Dharma talks, and by their always wonderful comments.

To Roshi.

Contents

Introduction ix

Case 1 Shakyamuni Buddha 1
Case 2 Mahakashyapa 6
Case 3 Ananda 9
Case 4 Shanavasin 15
Case 5 Upagupta 19
Case 6 Dhitika 23
Case 7 Mishaka 27
Case 8 Vasumitra 34
Case 9 Buddhanandi 37
Case 10 Buddhamitra 41
Case 11 Parshva 44
Case 12 Punyayasha 46
Case 13 Anabodhi 48
Case 14 Kapimala 52
Case 15 Nagarjuna 56
Case 16 Kanadeva 59
Case 17 Rahulabhadra 64
Case 18 Samghanandi 68
Case 19 Samghayathata 73
Case 20 Kumaralata 76
Case 21 Shayata 78
Case 22 Vasubandhu 84
Case 23 Manorata 87
Case 24 Haklenayasha 90
Case 25 Simhabodhi 93
Case 26 Bashashita 96
Case 27 Punyamitra 99
Case 28 Prajñadhara 102
Case 29 Bodhidharma 104
Case 30 Hui-k'o 106
Case 31 Seng-ts'an 111
Case 32 Tao-hsin 116

Case 33 Hung-jen 119
Case 34 Hui-neng 123
Case 35 Ch'ing-yüan 128
Case 36 Shih-t'ou 131
Case 37 Yüeh-shan 134
Case 38 Yün-yen 138
Case 39 Tung-shan 141
Case 40 Yun-chu 144
Case 41 T'ung-an Tao-p'i 148
Case 42 T'ung-an Kuan-chih 151
Case 43 Liang-shan 154
Case 44 Ta-yang 157
Case 45 T'ou-tzu 160
Case 46 Fu-jung 163
Case 47 Tan-hsia 166
Case 48 Chen-hsieh 168
Case 49 T'ien-t'ung Tsung-chueh 170
Case 50 Hsueh-tou 173
Case 51 T'ien-t'ung Ju-ching 176
Case 52 Eihei Dogen 178
Case 53 Koun Ejo 181
Soto Zen Lineage Chart 184
About the Chart 188

Introduction

Zen Light is a study of the *Denkoroku, the record of Transmitting the Light,* translated by Francis H. Cook.

The author of the *Denkoroku* is Zen monk Keizan Jokin (1268–1325) who was of the school of Dogen Zenji and was his third successor. As recounted by Keizan, the *Denkoroku* is a collection of transmissions of the fifty-three ancestors. In many ways, Keizan is responsible for the state and structure of the Soto School of Zen as we know it today, for he did much to popularize Zen and make it available to a vast lay public in ways Dogen probably would not have approved of. Keizan did an amazing thing in the *Denkoroku*, he focused on the experience of enlightenment that *led* to transmission. The scenario and action of each koan have something like the following format:

1. The master asks the disciple a question. It is not an ordinary question. It is a koan, or a riddle, or a deep penetrating query that hints at the Absolute. Often the question or koan contains the answer, but it is hidden.
2. The disciple expresses his understanding. It is the job of the disciple to penetrate the koan and delve into the Absolute.
3. Sometimes it is necessary for the master to repeat the question or ask it in a different way. The master prods the disciple into the Absolute.
4. The disciple gives his answer.
5. The master confirms the disciple's understanding and "transmits" the Dharma, making the disciple his successor and the next ancestor.

Introduction

This is generally how koan study works. The *Denkoroku* is not ordinary koan study between a Zen master and one of his students. There are two major persons in each chapter of the *Denkoroku*. First is the current ancestor. Second is the disciple and successor of that ancestor.

The ancestor is the one who represents and "holds" or "contains" the entirety of the Dharma. The disciple is the one the ancestor "sees" as his successor.

The lineage begins with Shakyamuni himself, who selects Mahakashyapa as his successor. Mahakashyapa thus becomes the first ancestor of the lineage. Mahakashyapa then selects Ananda, and so forth through fifty-three generations to Koun Ejo. These are the Zen masters who embody and preserve the Dharma of the Buddha and completely transmit the Dharma to their successors.

At the end of this book I list the lineage in some detail, giving alternative names by which the ancestors are known. There is also a discussion of the meaning of the lineage.

In our Soto Zen tradition, the lineage continues from Koun Ejo down to Maezumi Roshi and his successor, my teacher, Bernard Tetsugen Glassman, Roshi. The lineage is similar to the apostolic succession of the Christian religion. However, there is a difference. The Zen lineage does not only include popes or Zen masters. In the Zen tradition, each person who receives the precepts, or *Jukai,* becomes part of the lineage. Part of the Jukai ceremony includes making a personal copy of the lineage chart (or Bloodline chart) beginning with Shakyamuni Buddha down to the present. In my case, for instance, one of the contemporary teachers listed is Maezumi Roshi, who was the teacher of Tetsugen Roshi. After Maezumi Roshi's name, there is Tetsugen Roshi's name and then he, as part of the transmission

Introduction

ceremony of Jukai enters my name in the next line of the lineage chart. Subsequently, I add the name of any student who will take the precepts, or Jukai, with me. Thus, the lineage extends to every individual who makes a public declaration of his or her commitment to follow the Way.

My study of the *Denkoroku* with my teacher, Glassman Roshi, took place over a period of about two years. I would work on each "case" and when ready, present my understanding to Roshi.

The major question that struck me as I studied each case was: "What is transmitted?" The title of the book told me: "Light." The Transmission of the Light. "Light" is a central metaphor in the *Denkoroku*. Keizan uses the term "Light" in much the same way Christians use the words Inner Light or Holy Spirit. Other terms or metaphors for Light are Buddha-nature, or The Unborn, the major metaphor of Bankei, a Zen master of the eighteenth century. As I was reading and studying the *Denkoroku,* at times I felt I was reading the words of St. John the Apostle, the writer of the Fourth Gospel and the Apocalypse, and sometimes I felt I was reading St. Paul.

I believe the major teachings of Zen and Buddhism are present in the *Denkoroku*. As I went deeper with each case, the teachings of the *Denkoroku* had a cumulative, powerful impact on me.

When I worked on the first case, Shakyamuni Buddha, the similarity between the case and a phrase of Meister Eckhart struck me: "The eye through which I see God is the same eye through which God sees me." I wrote a poem using these words. In presenting my understanding of the first case to Roshi, I also presented my poem. Roshi then asked me to write a poem for each case and make the poem

Introduction

part of my presentation. After completing my study of the entire *Denkoroku,* Roshi asked me to write down my poems and my understanding.

This book contains my thoughts on each of the koans of the *Denkoroku* as well as poems. I should warn the reader that my thoughts do not necessarily reflect the understanding I presented and that which was approved by Roshi. Rather, what you have in this book is commentary on the teachings found in each of the enlightenment experiences of the ancestors.

This is done for a very important reason. I believe koan study is a very personal thing, and I do not hold with the view that there is a specific answer for each of the various koans. I do not believe that there is a set answer for the koan *Mu,* or for Hakuin Zenji's great koan, "What is the sound of one hand?" I think each of us, as we sit and meditate and wrestle with these koans, will find a place of *Mu* within our beings. We will find the solitary hand that makes the sound within our being, and expresses the essence of our being. Put another way, I see koans as archetypes of experiences, common to all sentient beings, which are held deep in the collective unconscious, or *alaya vijñana,* as the old Buddhists would say. Zazen provides a pipeline which connects the inner self of each person into this vast reservoir of experience. In this way, we can connect with that which a koan presents. But the connection is our connection. The words are our words, our experiences. This is the way of koan study for me.

So please don't look for answers in this book, but rather for thoughts about the major teachings of Zen.

It is also my concern that these teachings be presented in non-technical, non-Buddhist, and non-Zen jargon so that they may be accessible and available for anyone who reads

Introduction

this book. This book is for the beginning as well as the advanced student of Zen. I also think the book may speak to the person who may never have opened a Buddhist book before, who may never have done zazen, or any type of meditation—a person with no experience in Zen Buddhism. So don't worry if you are one of these people. I trust that what is in these pages, hopefully will reach you, and may possibly have meaning for you.

Thank you, and may your life go well.

CASE 1

Shakyamuni Buddha

Shakyamuni Buddha saw the morning star and was enlightened, and he said, "I, and the great earth and beings, simultaneously achieve the Way."

Keizan's Verse
A splendid branch issues from the old plum tree;
In time, obstructing thorns flourish everywhere.

Thoughts

It seems to me that the ground of the faith and practice of Zen is in this first case. Shakyamuni Buddha declares conclusively that all sentient beings, indeed, all of creation, simultaneously have attained enlightenment. He includes *all* sentient beings. There is a significant difference between the translations of the *Denkoroku* offered by Francis H. Cook and Thomas Cleary. In the Cook version, as above, the translation reads, "I, and the great earth and beings, simultaneously achieve the Way." Cleary's version reads, "I and all beings on earth together. . . ." It's possible to stretch

Case 1

Cleary's translation to indicate that not only are all sentient beings enlightened and achieve the way, but all creatures and the great earth as well. On the other hand, the Cook translation can mean that all things, just as they are, right now, are perfect and complete, including all sentient beings, all rocks and trees and grasses and mountains and rivers and streams. Indeed, including the weeds!

Shakyamuni truly means all. He excludes nobody: the sick, the criminals, the rich, the poor, the blind, the beggars, the homeless, lawyers, politicians, blacks, whites, Asians, and Latinos.

Probably most people who will either read or hear these words are "liberals," by which I mean people who are mostly white, upper middle class; people with a "social conscience," interested in preserving the environment, opposed to capital punishment; those who support causes such as Amnesty International, Save the Whales, The Nature Conservancy, and generally vote the Democratic ticket. I am one of these people. Naturally, we liberals concern ourselves with just such a list: the sick, the criminals, the rich, the poor, the blind, the beggars, the homeless, the lawyers, the politicians, blacks, whites, Asians, Latinos. But wait a minute! Do we really want to include the rich in this list? How did they get in?

Somehow, the rich and powerful just don't seem to fit. They don't seem to belong. We feel differently about the rights of the poor than we do about the rights of the rich.

Before I became a Zen monk, I was a professional fund-raiser. During my fund-raising career, one of the positions I held was as director of development for the Center of Urban Affairs of the University of Southern California.

Shakyamuni Buddha

That's right, USC. The *alma mater* of most of the Nixon and Reagan administrators. The home base of white middle-class conservatism, if not Republicanism. What was I, a bona fide liberal, doing at USC? They hired me because they had created a new school, The Center of Urban Affairs, to reach out to the poor black neighborhoods that surround USC. For a separate school with its own dean, there had to be a fund-raiser whose main job was to identify a constituency, develop a board of counselors (like trustees, only on the individual school level), and ultimately, raise funds needed to support the school. Given the nature of the programs and policies of The Center of Urban Affairs, nothing but a bona fide liberal would do. I was that liberal.

One day, on one of my fund-raising forays, I was sitting on the other side of the desk of a prominent chief executive officer in the oil industry. I was recruiting him for our board. This was during the Nixon years and just after Vice President Spiro Agnew—who, during his heyday, had been the scourge of liberals everywhere—resigned from office in disgrace. The man I was recruiting had hired Mr. Agnew, much to the dismay of liberals.

During our visit, my host received a phone call. I knew from his end of the conversation that the person he was speaking to was Mr. Agnew. I also knew that I had to make an appropriate and probably flattering comment about the situation. Finally the phone call ended. My host replaced the phone in its cradle, looked at me, and asked, "Do you know who that was?" "Yes," I responded, "it was Mr. Agnew, and I must say, it really was a wonderful thing for you to give him a job, just at the time when he was in disgrace and shunned by all."

Case 1

My comment was satisfactory. I gained another prestigious member for our board of counselors and a fat check.

Afterwards I felt dirty. I felt I had prostituted myself. If I had told my prospect just what I really thought of Mr. Agnew, I would never have gotten him to join our board, nor would I have gotten the check. I would have felt good if my prospect had given a job to an ex-convict of any description, even someone who had committed murder, or armed robbery, or just about anything—any criminal who had paid his or her debt to society and needed a job. That would have been all right. But was it? Why was *that* all right, and why was giving a job to Mr. Agnew not? I then realized my "liberal bias." I saw my prejudices against the rich, the powerful, the wealthy. I didn't know then that Shakyamuni's enlightenment included them, too, and that all beings, everyone—including the rich, the powerful, the wealthy—are right now, simultaneously, perfect and complete, just as they are!

Keizan's verse makes this implicitly clear by declaring "the splendid branch" as well as "obstructing thorns"—the good and the bad, the whole and the cripple, the blind, the beggars, the homeless, the poor, the rich, the privileged, the dictators, the criminals, the absolute, the relative, the yin, the yang, all together, form the one body of creation. One sees the depth and beauty of Roshi's contribution to my poem "All together—One flavor."

I also feel the word "simultaneously" includes all times, not just the present. All beings—past, present, and future—are in the simultaneous moment of Shakyamuni's enlightenment.

Shakyamuni Buddha

Shakyamuni realized this tremendous reality when he saw the morning star. Here is the first declaration of the ground of our faith. This is the first use of the metaphor of Light. The Light of the morning star. The Light that is the ground of enlightenment. The Light that is, from this moment on, transmitted from master to disciple—teacher to student—to the present.

The teaching contained in this first case is that all beings are enlightened. All beings are the Light. All beings are Shakyamuni Buddha. All beings are complete. All beings are, to use a Christian word, "saved." Not that all beings contain or have a glimmer of the Light within them. They have the Light entire and complete. Not that all beings "contain" the Light. They *are* the Light. Everyone. No exceptions. This is the enlightenment experience of Buddha: the Light that he perceived within himself—that burst within him and is transmitted from master to disciple.

Poem

Shakyamuni Buddha
(After Meister Eckhart)

The Buddha eyes that see me
Are the same eyes that see the Buddha

The heart that beats within the Buddha
Is the same heart that beats within me.

"All together—One flavor"

CASE 2

Mahakashyapa

The first ancestor was Mahakashyapa. Once, the World-Honored One held up a flower and blinked. Mahakashyapa smiled. The World-Honored One said, "I have the Treasury of the Eye of the True Dharma and Wondrous Mind of Nirvana, and I transmit it to Mahakashyapa."

Keizan's Verse

Know that in a remote place in a cloud-covered valley,
There is still a sacred pine that passes through the chill of the ages.

Thoughts

Enlightenment and transmission take place instantaneously, like the lightbulb that flashes above the head of the cartoon character who says, "I've got it!" You may strive and strive for hours, days, years, until at a particular fraction of a moment—a fraction so small it is beyond measure—when for no apparent reason—bang! "That's it! I've got it! Now, I know! Why didn't I know before? It's so easy, after all! What a fathead not to have seen it sooner!" "Getting it" probably has nothing to do with formal training, or seeking, or study. It's hardly worth mentioning, so insignificant can the actual "means" of enlightenment be. Zen history has many stories of Zen masters who "realized it" in this way. Enlightenment is subtle. As subtle as a smile. So subtle it is easy to miss. It could be the holding up of a flower, the blinking of an eye, the striking of a pebble on a stick of bamboo, the overhearing of a verse of the sutras, the reflection of one's face in a mirror, the nudging of a cat wanting to be stroked.

This is one of the "secret" teachings of Zen. The secret is that there is no secret. The greatness of Zen is that it is not great. The magic of Zen is that there is no magic. Nan-ch'uan, a Zen master, in response to the question "What is the Way?" said it is "ordinary." Zen is not something that shakes the earth and causes mountains to quake. It is not some blinding Light that all of a sudden reveals all truth. The truth of Zen is in the most insignificant and ordinary details of life. The washing of dishes. The shining of a pair of shoes. The walk in the woods. The holding up of a flower. A smile.

To "get it" we need to be awake, aware, and alert. The Sanskrit word "Buddha" means to be awake. To be enlightened is to be aware, awake, present, not absent. Being present where one is. Being completely present. Whatever we do—doing it with both hands. Walking with both feet. All is within us. That is why we do zazen. Zazen is a practice that goes within. It helps stop distractions; everything that takes us away from ourselves. It takes us to, and allows us to focus, within. To turn to the Light within. To turn to the Unborn, to Buddha-nature, to the Holy Spirit.

Case 2

We need not go outside our own personal experience. We need not read the great books. We need not listen to the great teachers. We need not climb the great mountains, make pilgrimages to the holy places. The holy places, the great teachers, the great mountains—all are within us. Zazen is a raft that takes us there.

Poem

Mahakashyapa

Sitting with the flower
Blackie, the cat, pokes his head
in my universal hands
nudging to be caressed.

I stroke his head.

He stretches
paws on my rakusu
looks wide-eyed in my eyes.

Old Shakyamuni
blinks.

And
Mahakashyapa smiles.

Case 3

Ananda

The second ancestor was the Venerable Ananda. He asked the Venerable Mahakashyapa, "Elder Dharma brother, did the World-Honored One transmit anything else to you besides the gold brocade robe?"

Mahakashyapa called, "Ananda!" Ananda replied. Mahakashyapa said, "Knock down the flagpole in front of the gate." Ananda was greatly awakened.

Keizan's Verse
Wisteria withered, trees fallen, mountains crumbled—
Valley streams gush forth, and sparks pour out from the stones.

Thoughts

After the Buddha's death, his followers held a conference. One of the important items on the agenda was to recite, remember, and record the teachings Shakyamuni Buddha gave during his forty years of teaching.

The chief monk was Mahakashyapa. Another of the leading monks was Ananda. Ananda was special for two

Case 3

reasons. First, he had been the Buddha's attendant for over twenty years and was very close to Buddha. Second, he had the gift of a photographic memory. He had only to hear a thing said once—no matter how long or complex—and he could repeat it word for word. Therefore, Ananda was a great resource person at this first conference of Buddha's followers.

Mahakashyapa asked Ananda to recite the Buddha's teachings. Ananda "ascended the seat" and began to speak. He began with the famous words, "Thus have I heard..." and recited a teaching of the Buddha. Ananda's words became known as the "sutras" because in those times books were stitched (or sutured) together. Each sutra or story or teaching of the Buddha begins with the words "Thus have I heard...."

Many days later, after Ananda had finished his recitation, Mahakashyapa asked the other disciples: "Is this different from what the Tathagata preached?" "Tathagata" is a sort of nickname people used to refer to Buddha. It means the Thus Come One, or The One Who Has Come (and attained enlightenment).

The disciples said, "It does not differ by as much as a word from what the Tathagata preached." With one voice they said, "We don't know whether the Tathagata has returned or whether this was spoken by Ananda." They continued and said, "The great ocean of the Buddhadharma has flowed into Ananda. What Ananda has spoken is the flowing, right now, of what the Tathagata has spoken."

While Ananda was quoting the Buddha's words, somehow they no longer were the Buddha's words, but had become Ananda's. The words flowed not from Ananda's brain but from his heart. Somehow, during his recitation, Ananda had made the Buddha's teachings his own.

Before that time he had been the attendant of Shakyamuni Buddha and had heard all the Buddha's teachings. But they weren't his. They were Shakyamuni's. There's a famous saying about hearing another's teaching: To hear and to quote someone else's teaching is like counting someone else's money while not having a penny of one's own. Most of us do that. We count the money of others and have none of our own. What good does it do us to count thousands of somebody else's dollars when we don't have a dollar of our own? We speak the words of others instead of finding our own.

This reminds me of the koan or story about Gutei's finger. Gutei was a Zen master famous for responding to every question by holding up a finger. "What is the meaning of life?" Gutei would hold up a finger. "What is the most important thing I must do right now?" Gutei would hold up a finger. "Is there a God?" Gutei would hold up a finger. No matter what the question or the situation or the problem, Gutei's answer was to hold up a finger. He was famous for this gesture. Gutei's Zen was "One-Finger Zen."

One day, a visiting monk, who was new to Gutei's monastery, asked Gutei's young attendant about his master's teaching. The attendant held up a finger. Gutei heard about this. Later, he met his attendant and asked him about it. The attendant held up his finger and Gutei cut off the tip of the finger with a knife. The attendant screamed in pain, holding the cut finger, and ran away. Gutei called

Case 3

after him. The attendant turned and looked at Gutei. Gutei smiled and held up a finger. And the attendant was at that moment enlightened!

There's also a story about speaking another's words in the *Journal of George Fox*. The founder of Quakerism, Fox had the habit of visiting different churches every Sunday, listening to the sermon made by the preacher and challenging the understanding of the preacher. On one of these visits, a preacher was quoting from the Bible: Paul said so and so, and Jesus said so and so, and Isaiah said so and so, and Moses said so and so.

"Wait a minute," interrupted Fox, "what do *you* say?"

The point is we need to find our own money. We need to find our own treasure chest. We need to find our own words. A German theologian of the nineteenth century named Blumhardt said, *"Jeder Mensch ist ein besonderes Wort Gottes."* "Each person is a special word of God." We need to find that word. Deep in the heart of our heart is that word. We need to find it and be able to express it. Zazen is a practice that helps us get to the place where the word within us lives.

One student told me about an experience she'd had with a twelve-year-old boy who was writing a report on Zen Buddhism. He knew she was a Buddhist and asked her to help him. She found the experience of finding words that he could understand to be exhilarating.

Shakyamuni spoke to people according to "their condition." He used words that would meet their condition. When he met a farmer, he would speak in farmer's terms. When he met a person who was highly versed in the old Indian scriptures, the Vedas, he would speak to them using their knowledge of the Vedas.

Ananda

There's a story about one of the monks who was with Shakyamuni. This monk was retarded. He wanted to become enlightened like the others. So he came to the Buddha and told him so. "OK," said the Buddha, "I'll tell you what you have to do. Sit down in the opposite corner of the room. I'll roll a ball to you. You catch it and roll it back to me. We'll do it three times and after the third time you will be enlightened." "Oh, really?" said the monk. "Yes," said Shakyamuni. So they sat in opposite corners of the room and Shakyamuni rolled the ball to the monk the first time. The monk caught it and rolled it back. Shakyamuni rolled the ball the second time. The monk caught it and rolled it back. Shakyamuni rolled the ball the third time. The monk caught it and was enlightened!

What happened here? I believe Shakyamuni Buddha saw the faith of the monk. And because the monk's faith was so intense and so pure, he was enlightened.

Ananda's patience was incredible. Ananda probably joined Buddha's group while in his twenties. He stayed with Buddha as his attendant for twenty-five years. Ananda was not to be the Buddha's successor because he had not yet found *his* word. Mahakashyapa, the chosen one, had found his word. Ananda subsequently was Mahakashyapa's attendant for twenty more years before he attained enlightenment. So he patiently studied and persevered for forty-five years before he was enlightened!

Throughout this entire period Ananda lived a life of selfless service, always with joy and never complaining. The name "Ananda" means "joy."

What a wonderful person he must have been! A life of complete service, and then he reached that point in his life when bang! he was ripe. Shakespeare said: "Ripeness is

Case 3

all." At that point, everything came together for Ananda. He had found the word and now the word was his own.

I'm not saying the words and teaching of others are not important. I'm not saying the sutras, the Bible, the Koran, and all the holy books are not important; that we should not read them. I am saying the teachings of the sutras need to be visible in our lives.

But now I will go a step further. Zen teaches that the sutras and all the holy books are really not necessary. The sutras and all the holy books are within us, and we have access to them. We can reach them in zazen.

Poem

Ananda

Kashanda
Anakasho
Tettsumui
Muitettsu
No robe
No sleeve
No Mahakashyapa
No Ananda
No pole
No gate
No Tetsugen
No Mui
No No
Yes

Case 4

Shanavasin

The third ancestor was Shanavasin. He asked Ananda, "What kind of thing is the original unborn nature of all things?" Ananda pointed to a corner of Shanavasin's robe. Again, he asked, "What kind of thing is the original nature of Buddha's awakening?" Ananda then grasped a corner of Shanavasin's robe and pulled it. At that time, Shanavasin was greatly awakened.

Keizan's Verse
Sourceless stream from a ten-thousand-foot cliff,
Washing out stones, scattering clouds, gushing forth,
Brushing away the snow, making flowers fly wildly—
A length of pure white silk beyond the dust.

Thoughts

In this case, Shanavasin asks Ananda for the uncreated, the unborn, for the Absolute—for the moon. He asks Ananda to reveal the secret of the universe, the glue that holds it all

Case 4

together. Is he testing Ananda, daring Ananda to show him that he can't show him? Or is he expressing his deep inner yearning, indeed, the yearning of all people, of all ages, past, present, and future? The last words of a moving and shattering play by Henrik Ibsen, *Ghosts*, are, "Mother, give me the Sun." After screeching these words, the son becomes incurably insane. Like the moth circling, circling the darting perilous flame, there is only one way to get it, and that way is to lose it forever. The great T'ang poet Li Po drowned, trying to embrace the reflection of the moon on a lake, from his boat. Give me the flame. Give me the secret of the unborn, the uncreated essence of all things. Give me the sun. Give me the moon.

Ananda is no fool. He knows that the passion of the moth will lead to a flaming deathblaze. He knows that the longing for the moon—the reaching out for the moon—can only lead to lunacy. Moonacy. So, he points with his finger at the moon. The finger of the moon points back. Indeed, the finger itself *becomes* the moon. The speck of dust on the *rakusu* (or vest) of Shanavasin is the totality of the moon, the uncreated, the unborn. Shanavasin has only to see it. He doesn't. So Ananda makes it clearer by pulling on the *rakusu*. Then Shanavasin sees and knows forever.

There is a well-known story of the Zen student who mistakes the finger pointing to the moon as the moon itself. The finger is not the moon. The finger is the finger and the moon is the moon. But is it? Is the pointing finger (contrary to the teachings of Zen masters of the past, present, and future) the moon itself? How can the pointing finger be the moon? Ananda knows. Shanavasin knows. It is the "pure white silk beyond the dust."

Poem

Shanavasin

Pointing to the rakusu—the moon
Grasping the rakusu—the moon

Pointless cry of all beings
throughout space and time

"*Mother! Give me the moon.*"

Mother! Give me the moon!

CASE 5

Upagupta

The fourth ancestor was the Venerable Upagupta. He attended Shanavasin for three years and then shaved his head and became a monk. Once, the Venerable Shanavasin asked him, "Did you make your home-departure physically or in spirit?" The master replied, "Truly, I made my home-departure physically." The Venerable Shanavasin said, "How can the Wondrous Dharma of the Buddhas have anything to do with body or mind?" On hearing this, the master was greatly awakened.

Keizan's Verse
House demolished, the person perished,
  neither inside nor outside,
Where can body and mind hide their forms?

Thoughts

The Buddha Way is a way of unity. The Way is a way that transforms from many to one. The Way heals the wounded, conflicted, body and mind. The Way reveals body and mind as not body and mind but BodyMind—mindbody.

Case 5

One—not two—not two—not one. It is beyond number. Gassho: the palms of both hands clasped together is the potent symbol of the Way. Two join as one.

The way of the world, however, is a way of distinctions and separations, multiplicity and delusions. We live in a world of delusions. The great delusion is that we are separate and distinct. Our senses do not discern beyond distinctions.

Zazen is a practice by which we can. The sixth ancestor, Hui-neng, defines zazen as the non-separation of subject and object. To understand this definition, consider what happens when one learns to play a musical instrument. I play the recorder. When first learning, there are many things to consider. There is the recorder itself, with its eight holes. There are the fingertips that cover the holes. There is the music sheet, with black notes on five lines and four spaces, and below and above the lines and spaces. Somehow all of these separate entities need to be together. At first what comes out of the recorder is bits of squeaks and strident sounds. It takes much practice to get the fingers to cover the holes so that a pure sound emerges from the recorder. Then there is the matter of relating the stopping of the holes with the notes on the sheet of music. Eventually, after many hours, days, months of practice, one approaches something almost pleasant to listen to. Eventually, one forgets the notes on the music sheet, the holes in the instrument, the fingers covering the holes. Eventually, one just plays. Eventually, one can call it music. Now turn to great master musicians like Charlie Parker and Dizzy Gillespie. Listen to the duets they play together in their early recordings like *Salt Peanuts* or *Ornithology*. All without sheet music. There is one sound. There is no separation between instruments and sheets of music. There is one sound. Music. Jazz.

Zazen takes place whenever we experience non-separation and realize unity; when we feel the pain or joy or anguish of another, even though there is no physical pain or joy or anguish of our own. When we empathize with another, we catch a glimpse of OneBody, as a mother knows when her baby hurts, even though no spoken communication takes place. Even when there is great distance between mother and child, the mother knows. The mother can feel the child's state of being from many miles away. This is particularly so in "simple" people, who deal directly with their feelings; the people who know in their bones what is happening to their loved ones, who know what the state of being is of anyone they meet.

This happens to us when we don't try to make it happen. We feel the "aura" of a group of people upon entering a room. We know what a person is really saying just by the "look" of that person even though their mouth is saying something else.

Our senses are treacherous. They lie to us. We must live with that lie and nevertheless make our lives work. With our vision, for instance, we see things topsy-turvy, and so we train our minds to turn vision around so we can make the upside-down world work for us. Our senses are not enough. Our HeartMind needs to inform them. When that happens we enter the realm of OneBody.

OneBody happens when we feel with one another.

Case 5

When we have compassion for one another. When we love one another. When we give to another. Every gift we make to another is a gift of OneBody. That's why the old Buddhas say there is no giver or receiver or gift—there is just giving.

Poem

Upagupta

*As Shylock could not cut
a pound of flesh without
a drop of blood*

*So Upagupta could not
leave home physically
without leaving mentally.*

*When the house is broken
and the people gone
there is no BodyMind to find
and no forms to hide.*

CASE 6

Dhitika

The fifth ancestor, Dhitika, said, "Because one who makes his home-departure and becomes a monk is a selfless Self, is selfless and possesses nothing, and because the original Mind neither arises nor ceases, this is the eternal Way. All Buddhas are also eternal. The Mind has no form and its essence is the same." Upagupta said, "You must become thoroughly awakened and realize it with your own mind." The master was greatly awakened.

Keizan's Verse
By acquiring the marrow, you will know the clarity of what you found;
Lun-pien still possesses subtleties he does not pass on.

Thoughts

"The Song of the Jewel Mirror Awareness" is an important poem in Zen literature. One of the things it says is, "Just to depict it in literary form is to relegate it to defilement." The

Case 6

Way is not a way of theories or dogmas or religious principles and practices. It is not a matter of philosophy or theology. We think we can "understand" the Way. We think we know what we are talking about when we talk about Zen. But to talk about it is to miss it. "The meaning is not in the words," says the "Jewel Mirror." Words are in the words. We think we understand what happens when we practice zazen. We sit, rather uncomfortably often, with much pain in our legs. We follow our breaths, or we count our breaths. We lose count. We go back to one. We experience the wonderful process of purification and believe we understand. We knock our heads against the rock of our koans. We think we've gotten it, that we understand it. But do we? Is it possible to "know" anything? The trouble with thinking we "know" something is that "knowing" is a position. We unconsciously, and automatically, reject anything that differs from our position. Can we ever hold anything still enough to say "This is it!"? If everything changes, can one "know" anything? Is it even accurate to use the names we use for people, places, things? Aren't names temporary handles? For instance, when I use the name Stefano, am I speaking of the person who is at this moment writing these words? Or am I speaking of the person who was the director of development of the University of Southern California in 1978? Are these two people the same Stefano? I understand that the cell structure of our entire body goes through a complete regeneration every seventh year. The very physical cell structure of the Stefano of 1978 is completely different from the one of 1995. In fact, the Stefano of 1995 even has a new name: Mui. The Stefano of 1978 was a Quaker. Mui is a Buddhist. The list

Dhitika

of changes between the two is endless. So when we say Stefano or Mui, or John or Mary, we should realize we are using temporary, provisional, and highly inaccurate handles or names. We should not presume we know the person we are talking to, or about, because of the continual changes that have and will take place in that person.

Science is another example of change. My wife, Margaret, is a medical provider, a physician assistant, specializing in AIDS work. She informs me that medical procedures, and even medications, that are known and proven one year are superseded the next because of new research. In the AIDS field there are major changes in the understanding and practice of medicine all the time.

Notknowing then becomes a pragmatic position to take on any issue. That's why the best way to know is not to know. Notknowing is the state of openness. When we don't know, there's space for anything to happen—even miracles such as the virgin birth of Christ, or the many miracles ascribed to Him. There is a wonderful poem, written by Tung-shan, the thirty-eighth ancestor (case 39). It is called the "Song of the Jewel Mirror Awareness." The poem contains two remarkable lines:

When the wooden man begins to sing,
The stone woman gets up to dance.

How can a wooden man sing? How can a stone woman dance? How can a virgin give birth? How can a single basket of fish and a few loaves of bread feed five thousand people? How can mountains move? How can rivers be still? How can bridges flow? In the state of notknowing, it all can happen—could have happened and will

Case 6

continue to happen. But "knowing" leaves no space. "Knowing" is a position that says that only what can fit in this little box of "knowing" is the way it is and nothing else will do.

The German mystic Meister Eckhart put it this way: "A poor person is one who knows nothing. One must be so empty of all knowledge that one neither knows nor recognizes nor senses that God lives in one. Further yet, one should be empty of all recognition that lives in one."

Poem

Dhitika I

Mu
Not Mu
Missed!

Dhitika II
(Three Treasures Mu)

Mu	*Mu*	*Mu*
Mu	*Mu*	*Mu*
Mu	*Mu*	*Mu*

Dhitika III

The greatest recipe
is not equal to
a crust of bread

CASE 7

Mishaka

The sixth ancestor was Mishaka. Once, the fifth ancestor said to him, "The Buddha said, 'Practicing wizardry and studying the small is like being dragged with a rope.' You, yourself, should know that if you leave the small stream and immediately come to the great ocean, you will realize the birthless." Hearing this, the master experienced awakening.

Keizan's Verse
Even with purity like an autumn flood
  reaching the heavens,
How can it compare with the haziness of a
  spring night's moon?
Many people desire to find purity in their lives,
But though they sweep and sweep, their
  minds are not yet empty.

Thoughts

Two of the major points in this koan are the effort we make to achieve wisdom or perfection or enlightenment, and Keizan's wonderful poem about the hazy moon.

Case 7

During his long teaching career, Shakyamuni Buddha told stories about animals to illustrate his teachings. These stories are the *Jataka Tales*. One of the tales he told illustrates what "wisdom" means.

> A man had a field of seedling trees that needed watering regularly. He had to go on a trip and asked the king of a group of monkeys who lived in the forest whether they would take care of the seedlings for him. The king of the monkeys was eager to oblige since the owner was so kind to them. So the man went on his trip and the monkeys began watering. After many days, the king of the monkeys decided it would be best if they knew exactly how much water to give each tree, so he instructed his subject-monkeys to lift each seedling to see how dry the roots were and then to water according to the dryness of the roots. So the monkeys carefully pulled up each of the seedlings, inspected their roots, and watered as needed.
>
> While they were busy doing their tasks, a man came to the field and saw what they were doing. He went to the king of the monkeys and asked why they were pulling up the roots of each tree. The monkey-king told him of his plan. "You fools," said the man. "Don't you realize that by pulling the trees up by the roots you are killing them?" And the man observed that while the monkeys were doing the best they could, they lacked the wisdom with which to do their job.

How does one attain wisdom? Why was the man of the story wise and the monkeys not? Do we inherit wisdom? Is wisdom something we are born with? If so, why does it seem that some have it and others don't? Can we develop wisdom through a systematic course of study? Through diligent persistence?

Here's a Zen story.

Mishaka

An old Zen master met a monk who was deep in zazen-meditation. "What are you doing?" asked the Zen master. "I'm trying to become a Buddha," responded the monk. "Ah, I understand," said the Zen master. Later the monk saw the old Zen master sitting on the ground rubbing a stone across the face of a brick. "What are you doing?" asked the monk. "I'm trying to make a mirror out of this brick," said the Zen master. "You can't make a mirror out of a brick by rubbing it, no matter how hard or how long you rub," said the monk. "Ah," said the Zen master, "and neither can you make a Buddha no matter how long or hard you sit."

Keizan makes the same point in his poem. Though people "sweep and sweep, their minds are not yet empty." They have not yet achieved the state of *shunyata*, the state of emptiness.

What is wisdom and how does one get it? Let's try a definition. What distinguishes wisdom from intelligence, from knowledge? To put it perhaps Zen-like, I think the difference is that knowledge or intellect is the ability to know that one and one make two. Wisdom is the ability to know that one and one make three, four, eight, seventeen, or whatever. Wisdom is the ability to find the logical connection between illogical entities.

OK, so we have a somewhat working definition. How does one get wisdom? I don't know that we can "get" wisdom. It is "given." It is a "grace." It just happens. Why does it happen for some and not for others? I don't know. Wisdom is not absolute, in the sense that the person who has it always has it, or that the person who doesn't have it never has it. No. Wisdom seems to be elusive. Sometimes you have it; sometimes you don't. The greatest and wisest

Case 7

man can make the stupidest and silliest mistake. I think this accounts for the unfortunate fact that some Zen masters, and other religious leaders, sometimes slip into shabby, immoral personal behavior. I think this is due to a temporary lack of wisdom. A mistake we often make is permanently to endow a person with "wisdom," believing that everything coming out of that person's mouth is wise. No! We need to examine, weigh, and carefully evaluate each utterance, never giving up our inherent birthright that is, in some way, "wisdom." We should place whatever any teacher, priest, guru, pope, Zen master, or whoever says, against that "wisdom" in our own hearts, to see if deep within, it "clicks."

Is wisdom equal? Is it the same in all people? I don't think so. I think each person has wisdom in different degrees. Yet the wisdom within each person is "perfect." The wisdom of a fool is perfect. The wisdom of a Zen master is perfect. In that sense there is equality.

So what about practice? Polishing the stone. Sweeping and sweeping. Are we not to sweep our minds, clearing out the detritus that clutters our inner being? Are we not to engage in strenuous Zen practice? Is it all useless? Can we simply go on as we are, knowing that our inherent wisdom will guide us? If there is no point to Zen practice, i.e., if Zen practice cannot lead us to wisdom or any of the perfections, why bother? This is the deep question the great Zen master Dogen struggled with and his thunderous resolution was: *Practice itself is enlightenment*. We do not practice to become Buddha. We do not practice to achieve. We practice because we are Buddha. We do not practice to achieve wisdom. We practice because we are wise. Practice itself is wisdom. We do not practice with goals in mind. Practice itself is the goal.

There's a story about Zen practice. When one begins practicing, one realizes that mountains are mountains and rivers are rivers. Later, as one gets into practice and achieves initial insight, one realizes that mountains are not mountains and rivers are not rivers. Later, as one achieves enlightenment, one realizes that mountains are mountains and rivers are rivers. This is the meaning of such seemingly meaningless statements of Dogen, who would say something like "One cannot say mountains are mountains and rivers are rivers. One cannot say mountains are not mountains and rivers are not rivers. One can say mountains are mountains and rivers are rivers."

The Quakers have a lot to teach us. To the Quakers, the way one does things is as important as whatever end one wishes to achieve. "Process" itself is the Way. Nonviolence is not an end, it is a means. The means are the end. It is obvious we can achieve ends with violent means. Quakers say the means themselves determine the shape and character of the end. That's why it is crucial to Quakers that what they do is consistent with whatever they hope to achieve. Some may argue, this takes too long. All the major achievements of humankind have been made through force, legislation—the imposition of the will of the majority upon the reluctant minority. This is the quicker and practical way.

But I wonder, how true is this? Take the issue of slavery. Slavery had been a blind spot in the history of civilization for centuries. Everyone owned slaves—even Quakers.

Case 7

It took Quakers a good hundred years to abolish slavery completely amongst themselves. Quakers waited until they were completely united, in every individual local Monthly Meeting of Friends, throughout the country, on the issue of slavery. Finally, all together, they repudiated this heinous practice. One hundred years! Truly a long time, and yet they gave up slavery one hundred years before the rest of the world! So who was slow and who was fast? And they did it by "friendly persuasion" of each other.

And now the "hazy moon."

One of the mistakes we make is to think the goal of practice is to get to a perfected state of being. To become an *arhat*. To attain a "pure" mind. To find inner peace. To find perfection. This, we think, is Nirvana.

The hazy moon of Keizan is the state of imperfection, the state of living in the world as it is. Nirvana is not the pure moon where everything is perfect. The hazy moon is Nirvana. Nirvana is right here, right now, imperfect though it may be. Paul's complaint to Jesus is appropriate. He prayed to remove a major imperfection he had. Jesus' response was "No—in thy weakness is my strength."

Our attempts to achieve purity are not wisdom. The very attempt indicates wisdom is lacking. Purity is not the goal. The hazy moon—or that which is shrouded in the normal, everyday experience of living with imperfections—is the goal. We need to accept ourselves as imperfect human beings. Enlightenment lives in our imperfections.

In a lighter vein, Robert Herrick makes a similar point in his poem "Delight in Disorder."

Mishaka

A sweet disorder in the dress
Kindles in clothes a wantonness:
A lawn about the shoulders thrown
Into a fine distraction:
An erring lace which here and there
Enthralls the crimson stomacher:
A cuff neglectful, and thereby
Ribbons to flow confusedly:
A winning wave, deserving note,
In the tempestuous petticoat:
A careless shoe-string, in whose tie
I see a wild civility:
Do more bewitch me then when art
Is too precise in every part.

Poem

Mishaka

A great wave reaches
for the hazymoon
and for one brief moment
lives to die

CASE 8

Vasumitra

The seventh ancestor was the Venerable Vasumitra. He placed a wine vessel before the Venerable Mishaka, bowed, and stood. The Venerable Mishaka asked him, "Is this my vessel or yours?" The master thought about it. The Venerable Mishaka said, "If you think it is my vessel, it is your intrinsic nature; if you think it is your vessel, you will receive my Dharma." Hearing this, the master was greatly awakened concerning the unborn intrinsic nature.

Keizan's Verse
Just as an echo follows when a bell sounds on
   a frosty morning,
So, here, from the first there is no need for an
   empty cup.

Thoughts

All the Zen masters say the best way to study with a teacher is with an empty cup. In this way, there is space for the teaching. However, if we come to the teacher with

Vasumitra

a full cup—with our opinions, our ideas, our theories, our knowledge, and so forth—then there is no space for teaching. I have been studying and practicing Zen for over thirty years, yet each time I enter the *Dokusan* Room, the room where the student meets privately with the teacher for individual study, it is necessary for me to completely empty my cup of thirty years of "learning." Then I am able to receive from my teacher.

This koan, however, goes one step further. It challenges us not only to empty our cup, but to throw it away. The koan challenges us to realize there is no cup. Even when we tenaciously hold on to the cup, it is not there. It is a delusion. It is a pernicious delusion to think we have accumulated thirty or more years of learning and that we know! The cup is a delusion that separates. If there is no cup, what is there?

Poem

Vasumitra I

The master drinks
the wine of essential nature

The Disciple drinks
the wine of Dharma

Now no need for master
Disciple or Dharma

The frosty morning
chills the bones

Case 8

Vasumitra II

Not mine
Not yours

The ring of the frosty dawn
chills the bones

CASE 9

Buddhanandi

The eighth ancestor was Buddhanandi. He met the seventh ancestor, the Venerable Vasumitra, and said, "I have come to discuss the truth with you." The Venerable Vasumitra said, "Good sir, if you discuss, it is not the truth; truth is not discussed. If you intend to discuss the truth, then in the end it is not a discussion of truth." The master realized that the Venerable Vasumitra's truth was superior and was awakened to the principle of the Unborn.

Keizan's Verse

The discussions by Subhuti and Vimalakirti did not reach it;
Maudgalyayana and Shariputra saw it as if blind.
If you wish to understand the meaning of this intimately,
When is some seasoning not appropriate?

Thoughts

There is a famous story about a man who was interested in the Buddha's teachings. He wanted to have some questions

Case 9

answered before he would follow the Buddha. He approached Buddha and told him just that. Shakyamuni told him to fire away. The man asked questions such as: "Is there a soul?" "Is the soul immortal?" "What happens to the soul when the body dies?" "Is truth eternal?" "Does the truth apply under all circumstances?" "Is the truth absolute or is the truth different according to circumstances?" In one version of the story it is said the Buddha responded with "noble silence." In another version, Shakyamuni responded by telling a story about a man who had been struck with a poison arrow. His friends immediately wanted to remove the arrow. The man stopped them, saying, "Wait. Before you remove the arrow, let's study it. Let's look at the feathers on the end of the shaft and so determine the tribe of the man who shot the arrow. Then let's study the shaft and type of wood used and in this way we can find out the family of the man who shot the arrow. Let's take a sample of the poison and discover exactly how to treat the injury with the correct antidote." "This is all well and good," said the Buddha, "but if we wait until we know the answers to these questions, the man will be dead. Better to act quickly, remove the arrow, and save his life."

Such questions asked of the Buddha would take years and years of explication, argument, discussion, explanation ad infinitum. One would still be left with speculative opinions. It's not that we can't eventually find satisfactory answers, it's that we are living in a state of emergency. We are hit today with sorrow, sickness, and death. We need to take direct action now to resolve the present danger we are in. We need to deal with what is before us right now. Such theological explication, interesting though it may be, takes

Buddhanandi

us away from dealing with what is before us. We find all sorts of ways to escape from dealing with the present. Paradoxically, we can even use Zen practice to escape from the now.

Some people dedicate their lives to Zen and yet their personal lives are a shambles. Their lives are boxes. One box of their life is their religious life. Another is their professional- or work-box. Another is their recreational-box. Then there is the at-home-box, et cetera. There may be a different person in each box. The one in the profession-box may be a sharp, cheerful, ambitious, and energetic person, easy to get along with, who will go far. The one in the recreational-box may be fiercely competitive, needing to win at all costs. The one in the Zen-box may be pious, meek, submissive. The one in the at-home-box may be a stern disciplinarian. Worst of all, the boxes don't connect.

In the Zen-box he or she may be able to maintain a sterling religious life—observing the precepts, practicing the *paramitas*, receiving *Jukai*, and so on. He knows all the right moves in the religious service. She knows all the chants by heart—both in Japanese and English. His zazen posture is solid as a rock; never the slightest movement of his body. Her responses to koan study are sharp. Yet in her at-home-box she may lead a fractured life. There may be a husband, wife, lover, or partner at home—miserable—because of the absence of the "Zen" partner. In some cases there really isn't a marriage or true relationship, and yet they are continuing to live within the framework of whatever they think they have. So they turn to Zen practice to escape from their non-marriage marriage.

How many of us live in boxes?

Case 9

Zen is a practice that unites rather than separates. Yet the box-liver's life is fractured. How is this possible? How is one able to leave unresolved problems behind and turn to a personal pursuit of Nirvana?

Jesus put it this way: "If before you bring your gift to the altar, you remember that you have a difference to settle with another, first, go to that other, settle your difference and then go to the altar."

Zen practice is not simply sitting on a pillow, chanting sutras, banging one's head against a stone koan, having *Dokusan* with one's teacher, and so forth. Zen practice is what is before us right now, whatever that may be. Zen practice is working on fractured relationships. Zen practice is washing the dirty dishes. Zen practice is not passing the beggar with outstretched hands on the street without giving him or her something. Zen practice is taking care of right now.

Truth is found in the now. Truth is the dirty dish, the unswept floor, the lonely husband, wife, friend, the unsettled arguments.

Poem

Buddhanandi

A slice of pizza
sprinkled with
crushed red pepper
Ahhhh.

Case 10

Buddhamitra

The ninth ancestor was the Venerable Buddhamitra. He heard Buddhanandi say:

Your speech is one with your intrinsic Mind,
And not even your mother and father can compare in closeness.
Your actions are one with the Way,
And this is what the Mind of Buddhas is.
If you search externally for a Buddha with form,
He will not resemble you.
If you want to know your intrinsic Mind,
You are neither one with it nor separate.

Upon hearing this, the master was greatly awakened.

Keizan's Verse
Do not say that speech and silence are involved with separation and concealment;
How can senses and their objects defile one's own nature?

Case 10

Thoughts

There are two famous stories that may help illustrate this case. The first is a koan. The student asked the master: "What do you do if you meet the Buddha on a road?" The master shouted: "You kill him!"

The second story is the Jataka tale of Angulimala. Angulimala was a murderer who killed his victims, cut off a finger from the murdered one's hand, and added the finger to a grisly necklace of fingers that he wore around his neck. The name Angulimala means "grisly necklace." He did this because he insanely believed he had to kill one thousand people to achieve salvation. He had killed 999 people, and the last person he met was Shakyamuni Buddha, who was walking along a road. He ran after Shakyamuni. Shakyamuni continued his normal pace without hurrying. But no matter how fast Angulimala ran, he could not catch up with the Buddha. Finally, exhausted with his efforts, Angulimala called and asked Buddha if he was some sort of magician since he was unable to catch him. The Buddha told Angulimala who he was and converted him. Angulimala shaved his head, put on robes, and became a devout and most wonderful monk. There is much more to this story but the point I want to illustrate is Angulimala's inability to catch up with the Buddha to kill him.

In the first koan the question is, what do you do when you meet the Buddha on the road? You kill him. In the second story, the Buddha is on the road. No matter how fast you try to get to the Buddha, you cannot catch him. You cannot meet him. It is almost as if the Buddha on the road is a phantom or a mirage. No matter how far you travel to that which you think is before your eyes, it recedes into the far distance, always eluding you. Is the Buddha a mirage? Is the one you see a phantom? Does the Buddha exist? Where is the Buddha?

Buddhanandi says, "Not even your mother or father can compare in closeness." Further on he said, "If you search externally for a Buddha with form, he will not resemble you." Buddhamitra, knowing this, never spoke or even walked. He said:

Father and mother are not close to me;
With whom am I most intimate?
The Buddhas are not my Way;
With what Way am I most intimate?

Poem
Buddhamitra
Dialogue between Mind and Consciousness

C: *Why can't I see you?*
M: *I am your seeing.*
C: *How close are you?*
M: *The face in the mirror.*
C: *Where are you when I hurt?*
M: *In the center of pain.*
C: *How can I find you?*
M: *Don't look.*
C: *Who are you?*
M:

C: *Uncle.*

CASE 11

Parshva

The tenth ancestor was the Venerable Parshva. He attended the Venerable Buddhamitra for three years without ever sleeping lying down. One day, the Venerable Buddhamitra was reciting a sutra and he expounded on the birthless nature of all things. Hearing this, the master was awakened.

Keizan's Verse
Turning, turning—so many sutra scrolls!
Born here, dying there—nothing but chapters and phrases.

Thoughts

James Joyce's *Finnegan's Wake* begins in the middle of a sentence:

> riverrun, past Eve and Adam's, from swerve of shore to bend of bay, brings us by a commodius vicus of recirculation back to Howth Castle and Environs.

The last words of the book are the beginning of the first words of the book, completing the sentence:

Parshva

> A way a lone a last a loved a long the

Structurally, the book is crafted as were the ancient sutras. These were copied on long strips of paper or cloth and rolled up on a spindle. One read the sutra as the scroll unwound from one spindle and wound up on another. Reading a sutra, therefore, required turning. In Tibet, there are hand-held sticks with little wheels on them containing the words of a sutra. Turning the wheel by hand turns the sutra. By beginning *Finnegan's Wake* in the middle of a sentence and concluding the book with the first half of that sentence, Joyce achieves the turning: "Fin-again."

Make the sutra your own. Make the words of the Buddha yours, as Ananda was able to do. Until the words are yours there is only the turning. Turn turn turn until the very turning becomes you. Until it is not the sutra or the wheel or the spindle or the riverrun turning. You are the turning the running river the spindle the wheel turning turning turning.

Poem

Parshva

Catch your sutra from the falling star,
and let it sleep in every pore.

Case 12

Punyayasha

The eleventh ancestor was Punyayasha. He stood with folded hands before the Venerable Parshva, and the Venerable Parshva asked him, "Where did you come from?" The master replied, "My mind does not go or come." The Venerable Parshva asked, "Where do you dwell?" The master replied, "My mind does not stop or move." The Venerable Parshva asked him, "Aren't you undecided?" The master replied, "All Buddhas are also like this." The Venerable Parshva said, "You are not 'all Buddhas,' and 'all Buddhas' is also wrong." Hearing this, the master practiced unremittingly for twenty-one days and acquired patience with regard to the non-origination of things. Then he said to the Venerable Parshva, " 'All Buddhas' is wrong, and they are not the Venerable." Parshva acknowledged him and transmitted the true Dharma to him.

Keizan's Verse
My mind is not the Buddhas, nor is it you.
Coming and going abide herein as always.

Punyayasha

Thoughts

This is a koan about abiding. It asks, where does one abide? In New York City? No! In an apartment? No! In the woods among the trees and animals? No! In the zendo? No! In a prison cell? No! In the heart? No! In the mind? No! In the teachings of Shakyamuni Buddha? No! Of Jesus Christ? No! Mohammed? No! Moses? No! Freud? No! Jung? No! The Beatles? No! Newt Gingrich? No! In the words of the Bible? No! The sutras? No! The Vedas? No! The Koran? No! The Talmud? No! If not in any of these, then where is our abiding? Let me illustrate with a poem.

Poem

Punyayasha

Jack and Jill went up a hill
to fetch a pail of water.
But there is no Jack, Jill, pail or hill.

Splashing water!

Case 13
Anabodhi

The twelfth ancestor was the Venerable Anabodhi. He asked the Venerable Punyayasha, "I wish to know the Buddha; what is Buddha?"

The Venerable Punyayasha replied, "You wish to know the Buddha, but he who does not know is the Buddha."

The master said, "Since Buddha is not knowing, how can I know that it is Buddha?"

The Venerable Punyayasha said, "Since you do not know Buddha, how can you know that it is not Buddha?"

The master said, "It is like a saw."

The Venerable Punyayasha replied, "It is like wood. Now I ask, what does 'saw' mean?"

The master said, "The Venerable and I are lined up evenly like the teeth in the saw. What does 'wood' mean?"

The Venerable Punyayasha replied, "You are cut through by me."

The master was suddenly enlightened.

Anabodhi

Keizan's Verse

The red of the rustic village is unknown to the peach
 blossoms;
Yet, they instruct Ling-yun* to arrive at doubtlessness.

Thoughts

As I indicated in Case 6, Dhitika, one of the "positions" in Zen is the "position" of "not-knowing." Unfortunately, this had become a cliché already in Anabodhi's time.

"Not-knowing" does not mean being ignorant. It does not mean not knowing. It means not-knowing. Not having any particular point of view. Being open to whatever happens. Being open to whatever may happen. Not evaluating things and making moral judgments on them. Just seeing things as they are without adding anything. Our tendency is to add things. I don't think it's possible not to add things to whatever we hear. Try an experiment. Say something to a group of five people and then immediately ask them to repeat what you told them. It is impossible that you will get five exact replications of what you originally said to them. Each person will add something. The problem is hearing. Hearing is complex. Whatever enters our "hearing" does not only enter our hearing. It enters our entire being. It is processed by everything we are, everything we have heard before. It is processed by our opinions, our experiences, our prejudices, our likes, our dislikes, our religious beliefs, our

---

* Ling-yun was a Zen master who arrived at enlightenment upon seeing red peach blossoms in full bloom.

Case 13

non-beliefs, our doubts, our anxieties. It goes through all of this muck. When it comes out again it is indelibly stained with all that we are. When we repeat what we hear, it is never the original something.

This is how gossip works. Gossip may not really be intentional. When we hear some bit of news and repeat it to another person, we can't help adding.

John phones his mother. "Guess what, Mom, I won the lottery."

"What? You did! Fantastic!"

"It was only third prize, and I had to share it with two million people, but I won a whopping twenty-four dollars."

Mama calls her sister Jane. "Guess what, Jane, John won the lottery."

"Wow," says Jane, "John is rich now."

"Sure," says mama, "he won the third prize."

Jane goes to the market and meets cousin Harriet. "Guess what, Harriet, cousin John won the lottery."

"Wow," says Harriet, "he's a millionaire. I guess he's gonna quit his job now and retire."

"You betcha. I know I would. First thing I'd do is go out and get myself a new car."

Harriet goes home and tells her husband, Jim. "Guess what, Jim, John won the lottery. He's quit his job and is going to buy that Mercedes he's always talking about."

Et cetera.

There's a wonderful play by Lady Gregory called *Spreading the News*, which illustrates this process beautifully.

Anabodhi

When Punyayasha replied to Anabodhi's question, "... he who does not know is the Buddha," he was not saying "not knowing" is the Buddha. Rather, he was saying that Anabodhi, himself, not-knowing, is already the Buddha. Anabodhi added to Punyayasha's answer and interpreted the opinion that "not-knowing" is the Buddha. So he missed.

Poem

Anabodhi

Not knowing if a tree falls
in the forest of the mind
saves the tree,
saves the mind.

CASE 14

Kapimala

The thirteenth ancestor was the Venerable Kapimala. One time the Venerable Anabodhi spoke of the ocean of Buddha-nature, saying, "Mountains, rivers, and the great earth appear in dependence on Buddha-nature. The three kinds of spiritual knowledge and the six paranormal powers appear as a result of it." The master, hearing this, was awakened.

Keizan's Verse
Even though the huge waves flood the heavens, how can the pure ocean water ever change?

Thoughts

This is a koan about Buddha-nature. How can I write about Buddha-nature? The great Zen master Dogen Kigen spent a lifetime writing about Buddha-nature. Another Zen master, Bankei, talked about the Unborn for all of his teaching life. Buddha-nature, the Unborn, the Absolute, the True Self, the Original Face, It, the Way, the *Tao*, the Light, the Inner Light, God, the Holy Spirit, Emptiness, *Shunyata*, Allah, Jehovah—all metaphors. And all miss the

Kapimala

point. Whatever we can say about it is not it. To say it is to miss It. It is something else. It is something more. It is something less. It is. It is not. The Soto Zen master Sekito Kisen wrote a poem called the "Identity of Relative and Absolute," or the "Sandokai," that says, "When you walk the way, you go no nearer, progress no farther." The Jataka story of Angulimala who tried to catch the Buddha told how no matter how hard he ran, he could never reach him. No matter how hard and cleverly we write about Buddha-nature, we cannot describe it. Semantically, it is both on the highest and the lowest level of abstraction. Somewhere in between. Nowhere in between.

I had an interview with a student at the prison where I teach zazen. The inmate-student was working on the first of the Four Great Vows of the Bodhisattva: "Creations are numberless, I vow to free them." This vow was the student's meditation subject, his koan. The question was, How can he free creations if they are numberless? The student had to show me how he would do it. He struggled and struggled with this koan for several weeks. Each time he entered the interview room (which in the prison doubles as a bathroom), he was off the mark, or didn't know what to answer. Finally, one evening, he came into the room and blurted out that he couldn't do it because he had to find the way to free himself first! "Right on," I said. Then he told me that that very morning after he had realized the necessity of freeing himself, another inmate with whom he was having trouble approached him and sneered, "I'm going to ruin your day." The student responded, "You can't ruin my day. Only I can ruin my day." He told me he didn't know

Case 14

where his words came from, but it stopped the other inmate, who remained speechless, and in some way they connected. "You know," the student-inmate said to me, "this stuff really works!"

Poem

Kapimala I
(Purification)

*One . . . two . . . three . . . four
. . . oops! a thought . . .*

*Back to
One . . . two . . . three . . . four
. . . oops!*

*One . . . two . . . three . . . four
. . . oops!*

*One . . . two . . . three . . . four
. . . oops!*

*One . . . two . . . three . . . four
. . . oops!*

Kapimala II

*When emptiness is struck
its beat reverberates in space—
and fills the space within the spaces—
the sun—the moon—the constellations.*

*I hear it in the swinging seas,
the tremble of the earth—*

Kapimala

*the walking mountains—
the swing of hills and valleys—
the grasses, weeds, the flowers—*

*I hear it in embracing trees—
the secrets of the forests—
the beings busy being born—
living, flying, dying—
the poetry of sages—
and in the beating of the heart.*

*Though there be earthquakes,
tidal waves and thunderstorms—
though there be forest fires, falling stars—
not an inch of earth, a drop of water,
a blade of grass, a touch of sky—
not a thought skips a single beat.*

Kapimala III
(A Slice of Purification)

One ... two ... three ... four ...
If only I had the faith to see what I do not see—

One ... two ... three ... four ...
Can this failing, aching body contain its cure?

One ... two ... three ... four ...
Can I compress the oceans to a drop?
the mountains to a pea?

One ... two ... three ... four ...
Not an inch of earth outside my heart?
Not a drop of water?

Case 15

Nagarjuna

The fourteenth ancestor was the Venerable Nagarjuna. Once, the thirteenth ancestor, Kapimala, paid a visit at the request of a Naga king and received a wish-fulfilling jewel. The master Nagarjuna asked, "This jewel is the best in the world. Does it have a form, or is it formless?" Kapimala replied, "You just understand having form and not having form, but you do not understand that this jewel neither has form nor is formless, nor do you understand that this jewel is not a jewel." Hearing this, the master was deeply enlightened.

Keizan's Verse
The orphan light, marvelously vast, is never
   darkened;
The wish-fulfilling mani-jewel shines
   everywhere.

Nagarjuna

Thoughts

More on Buddha-nature. Now it takes the shape of a pearl. A magic pearl that will grant one's every wish. A popular song of the 1940s and 1950s says,

When you wish upon a star,
Makes no difference who you are.
Anything your heart desires
will come to you.

The problem with this song, and with the wish-fulfilling pearl, is that our wishes have already been granted!

The Buddha tells a story about two men who spent the night in a hostel. One was very rich and the other very poor. The rich man decided to surprise the poor man. While the poor man slept, the rich man sewed a valuable pearl in the lining of the other's coat. Next morning he would surprise the poor man with his gift. The rich man went to sleep. Next morning, the poor man was not there. The rich man asked the innkeeper where the poor man had gone. The innkeeper didn't know. The rich man searched everywhere for the poor man. He couldn't find him. Eventually, he gave up his search and went about his way.

The poor man, in the meantime, was well away and continued his life as poor as ever. Things got worse. Often he went to bed very hungry. He spent many nights in deep despair, wishing for some stale bread to eat, wishing for something better. Many years later, by chance, the rich and the poor man met again. The rich man was overjoyed and told the poor man what he had done that night. The poor

Case 15

man was aghast. He turned his coat inside out, ripped apart the lining of his coat, and out popped the precious pearl. He had had it during all those years of poverty and despair!

And that's where we are. There is no need to make a wish. The wish has already been granted. It is dangerous to make a wish. It has been said that the problem with praying for something is, we always get exactly what we pray for!

We possess the pearl in the interstices of our being. The pearl is our true self. It is the inheritance we have already received.

Poem

Nagarjuna

*A beam of light
removes the clouds that
blacken the moon of
my frozen heart.*

*Minotaur defeated—
Secrets scorned
Triple poison neutralized—
Spider's web reclaimed—
A web of gold
A universe of pearls.*

*Oh, my heart!
Free!
Free!
Free!*

Case 16

Kanadeva

The fifteenth ancestor was the Venerable Kanadeva. He had an audience with the Great Being, Nagarjuna, in the hope of becoming a follower. Nagarjuna knew he was a man of great wisdom. First, he sent his assistant for a bowl full of water and had it placed before him. The Venerable Kanadeva saw it and thrust a needle into the bowl of water and presented it to Nagarjuna. They met each other and joyfully realized that they were of like minds.

Keizan's Verse
A needle fishes up all the ocean water;
Wherever fierce dragons go, it is hard to
   conceal themselves.

Thoughts

The last line of this koan, "They met each other and joyfully realized that they were of like minds," reminds me of a wonderful quote from George Fox. He said, "Meet one another in that which is eternal." This was the kind of

Case 16

"meeting" that took place between Kanadeva and Nagarjuna. No words spoken. They knew. Their "meeting" simply happened.

And what of the bowl of water? What of the needle? What is the bowl of water? What is the needle? Two become one. There is sexual imagery here. Sexual imagery and gender reversal in the teacher-student relationship is profuse and takes many forms, sometimes confusing.

1. *Gender reversal.* The teacher assumes the different roles of mother, lover, father, and spouse.

    The teacher as mother. The mother of the student carefully nourishes her son or daughter. First, she gives the newborn baby her own milk from her breast, because that is the only source of food the baby can digest at this early stage of development. Later, as the baby grows and develops into a child, the mother weans the baby away from her breast, and slowly introduces solid foods. At first the food is a light pudding or farina. As the child continues to be nourished and grow, the mother feeds the child more solid foods. Eventually the child becomes a young man or woman, and now the mother can offer dharma-meat.

    The teacher as lover. The teacher woos the student. The teacher showers gifts upon the student in the form of teachings he or she knows the student will easily understand and enjoy. The teacher entices the student with lovely stories of the dharma, like the *Jataka* tales. The teacher slowly and deliberately nurtures the relationship with the student so that the student grows to love the dharma.

The teacher as father. The teacher cares for the safety and well-being of the student. The dharma given to the student is carefully presented so as not to threaten the student. The teacher is aware of delusions which surround the life of the student and carefully protects the student. And so the teacher offers many toys and gifts of dharma which will lead the student away from the "burning house" of the three poisons of greed, hatred, and ignorance.

The teacher as spouse. The teacher joins the student in the student's quest for dharma, and encourages the student in whatever he or she encounters in the experience of the dharma. The teacher listens to the concerns, fears, doubts, realizations, of the student with an openness and spousal bias of acceptance, encouragement, and support.

2. *The student changes roles as lover, son, husband, and father.*

The student as lover. The student is stricken with love for the dharma, and follows the teacher and listens to the dharma taught by the teacher with total acceptance, with the bias of a lover.

The student as son or daughter. The student receives dharma from the teacher as a son or daughter would receive a gift from his or her father or mother. The student knows she or he can always

Case 16

turn to the teacher for whatever reason, in complete trust, knowing that she or he will always be received unquestioningly.

The student as spouse. The student joins with the dharma of the teacher in order to give birth to the realization of the dharma within himself or herself.

The student as father. The student carefully nourishes the dharma she or he has just given birth to, and allows it to slowly grow and develop into full bloom.

3. *The teacher is the mother who gives birth to the son or daughter.* The teacher sees that the student has realized the dharma within his or her being and, in the formal act of recognition of *Jukai*, gives birth to a new being by giving the student a new dharma name. The name will both describe the special characteristics of the student and be a standard of aspiration for the student.

4. *The teacher receives the lover, the student, and uniting, they become one body.* As the student matures in the dharma, the dharma-mind of the teacher and the student become one. Not that the student parrots the way and the words of the teacher, but that somehow, although different, they are nevertheless the same. In the ceremony of *Denbo* (transmission), there is a sequence in which the student places his or her *zagu* (bowing mat) over the *zagu* of the teacher, and both bow. Later, the teacher places his or her *zagu* over the *zagu* of the student, and both bow.

This is some of the stuff of transmission.

Kanadeva

One can see that sexual metaphor and imagery permeates the teacher-student relationship. One can also understand how easy it is for either teacher or student to fall into the trap of either exploiting one another, or physically engaging in sex. I think sex between teacher and student changes everything, and they are no longer able to pursue their dharmic relationship, for they have substituted sex for dharma.

Poem

Kanadeva I

needlemind
sticks my heart
now
every breath
a death

Kanadeva II

the needle
sticks the body
sticks the mind
sticks the water
sticks the seed
sticks the dragon

no outside-inside
no relative-absolute
no master-disciple

fused
yet different

Case 17

Rahulabhadra

The sixteenth ancestor was the Venerable Rahulabhadra. He was serving Kanadeva, and when he heard about karmic causes in former lives, he experienced awakening.

Keizan's Verse
*What a pity his Dharma eye was not clear.
Deluded about Self, repaying others, the
 retribution never ends.*

Thoughts

This case is about karma. Rahulabhadra's father had a garden. In it, a big ear of fungus was growing on a tree. The fungus was magical in that whenever they picked some, it grew again. Even when it was all gone, it regrew. Kanadeva visited Rahulabhadra and his father. They asked him about the fungus and Kanadeva explained that a long time ago a monk was given alms by the Rahulabhadra family. The monk, however, had not yet completely "opened his eye" to the Way. So the alms he was given were consumed in vain. When he died he became a mushroom to resolve the karma he incurred.

Rahulabhadra

Karma plays a very strong role in this case. The idea of karma is that everything we do, say, or think will result in a consequence or reaction at some time or other. Shakyamuni Buddha further refined this idea by saying that these acts must be *volitional* in order to result in karmic reaction. In this case, we are talking about the karma of monks. In Keizan's teaching about this case he says a monk—and this applies to any religious vocation—who is not sincere in his or her vocation makes karma that needs resolution. Keizan warns the monks in his care that those who turn to the religious life for selfish reasons, whatever they may be, fall into this trap of karma. The point, I believe, is that if we do good things for egoistic reasons, we pervert them. Keizan goes so far as to say that one becomes a "traitor" of the Way if one is in this state of egoistic vocation. This applies to all religious people who profit from their religious vocation, either egoistically, through the adulation they may receive from their students, or through financial profit. It is interesting that the Buddha prohibited the use of the Dharma to conduct a business.

Most religious orders include a vow of poverty in their Rule. Poverty applies not only to material things but to spiritual matters as well. The "poor in spirit" Jesus talked about are those who managed to put aside their egos and stand before Him, empty and open, so that Jesus may enter their hearts.

Let's look at this closely. Does this mean that one may not "own" anything? In the radical days of Shakyamuni Buddha and Jesus, yes, that's exactly what it did mean. I guess that's why the religious life included celibacy. It was

Case 17

not possible to lead a "homeless" life unless one was alone and unmarried. Marriage requires the accumulation of property to contain it. It means a house, furnishings, et cetera.

Is it possible to maintain a degree of poverty within marriage? I think so. The key would be nonattachment to both material and spiritual things. Not being attached to whatever it is we think we "own." Not being attached to whatever it is we have either intellectually or spiritually "achieved." Whatever it is we think we have, we should drop it. This reminds me of the Groucho Marx song, "Whatever it is, I'm against it!" Whatever it is, drop it! The problem with attachment and ownership is that they are delusions. The reality is that whatever it is we think we own, we do not. How can we say we "own" a house when the house itself is temporary? Consider the tragedies that occur daily from fires, hurricanes, earthquakes, floods, and other natural disasters. In an instant all we have can be wiped or blown away. The very land we stand on can give way and swallow us up. Realizing the impermanency of it all, nonattachment is the pragmatic way to go. We need to learn to live as if it could all be gone tomorrow. And it's OK.

I'm not advocating a life of penury, grimness, and tightness. Just the contrary. The Zen way is to live each moment to its fullest. Whatever you do, do with a full heart. Do it with enthusiasm and passion. Karma is the reason this way is pragmatic. Unless we follow the Way with an open heart, with poverty of spirit, without ego, we stand in danger of making karma that must be resolved at some time or other. We stand the risk of becoming a tree fungus—a mushroom—to be devoured by others until our karma has been expiated—completely resolved.

The Promethean myth echoes. Why was Prometheus tied to a stake and his liver nibbled at by a hawk? Was it because he stole fire for egoistic reasons? Was Prometheus sentenced for pride?

Poem

Rahulabhadra

Am I the monk
on the tree
eating the mushroom flesh
of past and present
karma?

Another Prometheus
tearing
my own liver?

Case 18

Samghanandi

The seventeenth ancestor was the Venerable Samghanandi. Once, Rahulabhadra said in verse,

Since I am without a self,
You should see the Self.
Because if you make me your master,
You will understand that the self is not the Self.

When the master heard this, his mind opened and he sought liberation.

Keizan's Verse
Mind's activity smoothly rolling on is the form the mind takes;
How many times has the Self appeared with a different face!

Thoughts

One of the great teachings of the Buddha is that all things are in flux. All things are impermanent. This is not hard for us to understand. We can see with our eyes and the rest of our

Samghanandi

senses that everything changes. From the moment we are born, our bodies change. They grow. Our minds develop. Our fingers develop. Our legs develop. We learn to crawl. To walk. To talk. Later we learn to drive automobiles. Then comes the time when our bodies begin to run down. In a previous case I wrote about the complete renewal the cell structure of the human body makes during the course of seven years. This probably matches the psychological changes that take place at the ages of seven, fourteen, twenty-one, twenty-eight, et cetera. The body I have now, at the age of sixty-six, is not the body I had at the age of twenty-one. That which I call my self and label, Stefano Mui Barragato, is not the same Stefano Mui Barragato he was at the age of twenty-one. Physically, he is completely different. Changes take place from moment to moment. The person I think I am today is a completely different person tomorrow. By tomorrow, many things will have changed in that which I call my self. There are many physical changes; cell structures that will have died and new cell structures that will have been born. Each day I am a new person. A new self.

So what we can say about the self, if we can say anything at all, is that the self is not constant. It is not a permanent entity. It is something that is constantly shifting and changing. We cannot point and say this is the self. Whatever we point at is no longer that which we pointed at; it is something different. The self is elusive. We cannot pin it down.

We therefore ask, what is it that we call the self? Is there something we can hold, keep still for a moment, and

Case 18

say, "This is it!" The Buddha teaches, "No, there is nothing that holds still." Even in the process of death there is movement. The body continues to decay until there no longer is a body. Dust and ashes. Not a trace remains of that which we called the body.

From this, one can begin to appreciate the great teaching of *shunyata*—emptiness. One can say the self is empty. Yet there is a body—elusive, changing, fickle, inconstant though it may be. There is a hand, eyes, ears, nose. There are houses, trees, cats, dogs, flowers, rivers, mountains. But they all have the same thing in common. They are in motion. They change. Never the same. That which I call a mountain is not a mountain. That which I call a river is not a river. That which I call the self is not the self. Mountains walk. Rivers are still. Bridges flow.

Words are treacherous. With language we try to fix things. We try to pinpoint things. We do very well at that. We do so well, we forget that everything changes. We forget, when we meet someone whom we haven't seen for years, that that person is no longer the person we knew. One of the major problems we have relating to one another is that we hang on to what we believe to be the self. We're constantly holding to ideas we have about one another. John is very funny. Jane is attractive. Joseph is selfish. Henry doesn't love his wife. "But I distinctly heard you say so and so, only just yesterday!" What one has said and believed in the past may no longer be the case. I can't say how often I have changed my mind about things. We are in flux, constantly changing, constantly developing, constantly progressing. Our preconceptions are obstacles to relationships.

Samghanandi

An examination of the human body and the cell structure with the powerful microscopes of today reveal larger and larger spaces. The closer we look, the more we see emptiness. The self is empty. That's why *shunyata* is so important. I believe *shunyata* is the best and most meaningful way to conduct a relationship. In emptiness, we are completely open to the other at this present moment. George Fox, the founder of Quakerism, said, "Meet one another in that which is Eternal." I say: Meet one another in emptiness.

Poem

Dialogue between Self and Emptiness

SELF:	*Knock Knock*
EMPTINESS:	
EMPTINESS:	*Knock Knock*
SELF:	
SELF:	
EMPTINESS:	
SELF:	*The aroma of incense.*
EMPTINESS:	*The sound of the heater.*
SELF:	*The feel of Margaret.*
EMPTINESS:	*The crick in the neck.*
SELF:	
EMPTINESS:	

Case 18

Samghanandi II

*self penetrating
the iron wall*

*no self penetrating
the iron wall*

*penetration
penetrates
penetration*

CASE 19

Samghayathata

The eighteenth ancestor was the Venerable Samghayathata. He served the Venerable Samghanandi. One time, he heard the sound of the wind blowing the bronze bells in the temple. The Venerable Samghanandi asked the master, "Are the bells ringing or is the wind ringing?" The master replied, "It is neither the bells nor the wind; it is my Mind that is ringing." The Venerable Samghayathata asked, "And who is the Mind?" The master replied, "Because both are silent." The Venerable Samghayathata said, "Excellent, excellent! Who but you will succeed to my Way?"

Keizan's Verse
Silent, still, the Mind rings and echoes in ten thousand ways—
Samghanandi, Samghayathata, and wind and bells.

Case 19

Thoughts

This koan seems to be the source of the similar famous koan in the *Mumonkan,* as well as the story Hui-neng tells in the Platform Sutra. Hui-neng was visiting a monastery and he met two monks who were arguing about whether the wind was moving the flag or the flag was moving the wind. He said it was neither the flag nor the wind moving. It was their minds moving.

Similarly in this koan, upon hearing the wind moving the chimes, is it the wind or the chimes moving? The answer is that it is neither the chimes nor the wind; it is the mind. Samghayathata said, "It is my mind." The next question is very significant. "Who is the mind?" Samghayathata answered: "All is silent."

There is no sound of bell, chime, wind, flag, two monks, Hui-neng, and no sound in mind.

Whatever takes place is inside. Whatever we see, hear, taste, smell, touch, is inside. I am sitting down, recording these words, looking at the trees through the window. What I see, I see in my mind. And the mind is silent. I hear the ticking of the clock as the pendulum swings back and forth. What I hear, I hear in my mind. The swinging is in my mind. When we see something outside, we separate. Separate from that which we see. As long as there is separation—the duality of here and there—we are in the realm of delusion. The great delusion is that there is something there.

But isn't this all nonsense? Isn't the clock ticking? The pendulum swinging? Aren't the trees outside beyond the window? The great Samuel Johnson ended all such mystic misconceptions by stubbing his toe on a rock and shouting

Samghayathata

"Ouch!" thereby proving the existence of the rock, his foot, and the pain. Did he really prove it? His foot hit the rock and he screamed, "Ouch!" At the very moment of impact, did anything exist but "Ouch!"? Wasn't that "Ouch" the very essence of unity? Did rock, foot, Johnson, or anything else exist but "Ouch!"? I think Johnson proved the fact of nonseparation between subject and object with his experiment. He proved it with his cry of "Ouch!"

Everything is "Ouch!" "Ouch!" is the entire universe. Ouch!

Poem

Samghayathata

no distance
between Samghanandi
Samghayathata
Hui-neng
Roshi
Mui

no distance between
beginningless beginning
endless end

silent
ringing of bells
ringing mind
ringing bells flag wind chimes

ting-a-ling-a-ling

Case 20

Kumaralata

The nineteenth ancestor was the Venerable Kumaralata. Once, the Venerable Samghayathata said to him, "Long ago, the World-Honored One predicted, "One thousand years after my death, a great being will appear in Tokhara who will inherit and promote the profound teaching." You have now met with this good fortune by encountering me." Hearing this, the master acquired the knowledge of former lives.

Keizan's Verse
*In past lives he cast off one body after another;
Right now, he encounters the Old Fellow.*

Thoughts

This koan presents Light. What form does the knowledge of former lives take within Kumaralata upon hearing the prophecy that his teacher Samghayathata makes? Keizan tells us in his poem. Casting away one body after another he meets the same Old Fellow. The same Old Fellow is the Light—the Light that shines throughout all time. The Inner Light that unites all humanity, all sentient beings, all things.

Kumaralata

This is the declaration of the nature of the Unborn proclaimed much later by Bankei. The Unborn illumines all creation. It is within each person and guides, teaches, and comforts. Keizan makes it clear that knowledge of past lives does not mean knowledge of past lives. It means all lives are present in the Light. The words "enlightenment" and "awakening" are translations of the Sanskrit word "Buddha." The Awakened One. The Enlightened One. To be Buddha means to live in the Light, to realize the Light that is within, and to reflect it. Not to cloud it over with our thoughts, ideas, preconceptions, opinions, knowledge, accumulation of facts and figures. To be awake is to be present in the Light. All things are present in the Light, just as they are. Even our mistaken notions are there. And our mistaken notions are enlightened!

Poem

Kumaralata

tick
tock

the old guy's light—
a single spark
in a square inch
of heart

and all the teachings
and delusions

hot winter
cold summer

tick
tock

Case 21

Shayata

The twentieth ancestor was the Venerable Shayata. Once, the nineteenth ancestor said, "Although you already have faith in the karma of the three times, still, you have not yet clarified the fact that karma is produced from delusion, delusion exists as a result of consciousness, consciousness results from ignorance, and ignorance results from mind. Mind is originally pure, without origination or cessation, without doing or effort, without karmic retribution, without superiority or inferiority, very still, and very intelligent. If you accept this teaching, you will become the same as all the Buddhas. All good and evil, conditioned and unconditioned, are like dreams and fantasies." Hearing this, the master grasped the deep meaning of these words and aroused the wisdom he had possessed since time immemorial.

Keizan's Verse
The camphor tree as always, is born in the sky;
Its limbs, leaves, roots, and trunk flourish
   beyond the clouds.

Shayata

Thoughts

The heart of this koan is karma and justice. The problem Shayata had is that his parents were devout Buddhists. They lived a very pious life, they did all the right things, and yet they suffered immensely during their life—they were poor, ill, et cetera. Their neighbors were outcasts—butchers, non-Buddhists, those who lived an immoral life—and yet they prospered.

Shayata's question is, "Why should the good ones suffer and the evil ones prosper?"

This is a timeless question. Why do the unjust prosper and the just suffer? Why are some people born poor and others born rich? Why the inequality whereby people are judged solely on birth and not on merit? One can hear the song of Tevya in *Fiddler on the Roof.* "If I were a rich man . . . Why couldn't I have been born—with a small fortune?" All the good things that could happen to Tevya and his family, instead of being poor and in misery, poverty and squalor! Why, he could even study the holy books and have a seat by the Eastern Wall. "If I were a rich man!"

In the days of Shakyamuni, the usual reason given for differences was karma. The idea of karma is that one's actions will produce equal and appropriate results. If one commits evil acts, one will reap evil results. However, since it didn't seem to be that way—since people who were evil were achieving good results—then karma must be carried over to future lives. A very complicated system of karmic results was devised. There are acts that will produce direct results in this life, acts that will produce results in the next

Case 21

life, and acts that will produce results in a third life. There are acts that will cause one to be reborn as a particular animal—the choice of animal depends on the exact corresponding act committed.

The idea is that justice will eventually triumph. Injustice will not. Those who, in this life, are unjust and commit evil acts will, in future lives, receive their just deserts.

The resurrection of Christ makes sense from the point of view of justice. Justice demands that Christ be resurrected. No other outcome is acceptable. Christianity is impossible if there is no resurrection of Christ. I believe Paul makes this very point.

Kumaralata's response to Shayata's question, however, is different. In Cook's translation of the *Denkoroku*, Kumaralata says, "Karma is produced by illusion." In Thomas Cleary's translation, the word is "confusion."

Cook's translation continues with an abbreviated "chain of causation." Illusion produces karma; illusion exists as a result of consciousness, consciousness results from ignorance, and ignorance results from mind. With the exception of the word "confusion," Cleary's translation follows the same pattern and words.

What does it mean that "illusion" is a result of "consciousness"? Is everything we are conscious of an illusion? How does consciousness result from ignorance? Ignorance from Mind? Then we have the great leap: Mind is originally pure—without origination, without cessation, without doing or effort. Without karmic retribution. Without superiority or inferiority. It is very still and very intelligent. Cleary translates: "Serene and spiritual."

Shayata

The late Shunryu Suzuki Roshi, of San Francisco, talked about Big Mind and Little Mind. It is Big Mind that is without origination or cessation, superiority, and inferiority. It is very still and serene and spiritual. Without karmic retribution. Little Mind is fraught with origination, destruction, doings, effort, retribution, victories, defeats, good and evil, and karma. Little Mind is the everyday mind we bring to our senses. It is Little Mind that causes ignorance. In Little Mind we see all things and conceive all phenomena as real. All we see—everything—is "outside." All is dualistic. Little Mind is dualistic mind. Little Mind separates subject from object. Little Mind sees the differences. Little Mind sees the unjust prosper and the just suffer. It is Little Mind that has created the complicated system of karmic retribution of past and future lives in which justice will take place.

Shayata points to Big Mind. All is still, in Big Mind. All is empty. In emptiness, there is no good or evil. There is no conditioned and unconditioned. All of these things are dreams and illusions. Dreams and fantasies. Karma does not exist in Big Mind.

Karma is wedded to justice. Big Mind is beyond justice. Big Mind is the state of serenity. The state of equanimity that is the state of emptiness. In this state no matter what happens, it's OK. There's nothing to eat today. OK.

I teach meditation at a maximum security prison. One of the points I have great difficulty getting across to the student-inmates is that whatever happens is OK. We practice in a spacious room. We had to go through handstands to get that room. The prison officials wanted to take

Case 21

it away from us and have us practice in another area. My attitude was, "Fine we can practice anywhere. We don't have to practice in this wonderful big room. We can practice in the hallway with other inmates passing by." I really believe this. I believe Zen practice does not have to take place in a beautiful zendo far off in the mountains, with very comfortable, matching *zafus* and *zabutons* (pillows and mats), with beautiful altars and images of the Buddha, subdued lighting, and wonderful equipment such as large beautiful-sounding Japanese bells. These are all trappings. These are all extras. I believe zazen can take place at any time and at any place. The sixth ancestor, Hui-neng, defines zazen as the nonseparation of subject and object. Where there is unity there is zazen. Where there is One-Body there is zazen.

This is very hard for inmates. They are in a maximum security prison and kept on a very tight string. There is very little space in a prison. Little outer space and little inner space. The larger inmates in our group even have a hard time fitting into their tiny cells. They want a place where they can have space. This is most understandable. And so we fought for our room and got our space. We have blankets instead of *zafus* and *zabutons*. Someday we may have *zafus* and *zabutons*. Shayata says that all of these things are dreams and fantasies. But they are nevertheless important. Yes, they may all be trappings. So, I'm not being consistent? So what? Who needs to be a "hobgoblin of little minds and divines"?

I come back repeatedly to Dogen's enlightenment experience on hearing his teacher, Ju-ching, encourage his students to drop body and drop mind. Drop whatever it is we have. Whatever it is we want. Drop our need for justice. Drop our antipathy to injustice. Drop our thoughts. Drop our poverty. Drop our riches. Drop our attachments. Let everything go. Drop whatever we need. Whatever we think we need is a delusion. Drop whatever we think we don't need. Whatever we think we don't need is a delusion. Deep is the teaching that our needs are delusions. Deeper still is the teaching that our delusions are the enlightened state itself!

Poem

Shayata I

a branch of the maple tree
in my garden
snaps in the wind
snapping the topmost branch
of the camphor tree
in China

Shayata II

I spotted a bird
busy building
a nest
high
in the branches
of the maple tree.
Squinting—a closer look,
I saw myself.

CASE 22

Vasubandhu

Shayata said, "I do not seek the Way, yet I am not confused. I do not pay obeisance to Buddha, yet I do not disregard Buddha either. I do not sit for periods, yet I am not lazy. I do not limit my meals, yet I do not eat indiscriminately either. I am not contented, yet I am not greedy. When the mind does not seek anything, this is called the Way." When Vasubandhu heard this, he discovered uncontaminated knowledge.

Keizan's Verse
The wind blows through the great sky, clouds
   appear from the mountain caverns;
Feelings for the Way and worldly affairs are
   of no concern at all.

Thoughts

This case concerns itself with our efforts to practice. Dogen Zenji says practice itself is the enlightened way. Many of us practice for the sake of achieving something. We want to achieve tranquillity of mind, peace of mind. We want to settle

Vasubandhu

our minds. We want to become Zen students, Zen teachers. We have objectives. This koan tells us that having objectives is not the Way. By having an objective we miss the Way. The reason we miss it is that there is nothing to attain. We already have it. Where is it? Within. Back to Keizan's metaphor of the Light. It is within. Within each person. If it's there already, why do we need to practice? Back to Dogen. We practice because we have the Way. Not to seek it. Not to find it. Not to gain tranquillity of mind. Not to gain peace of mind.

Why not try to gain peace and tranquillity of our monkey minds that devour us and drive us crazy with their tempestuous storms and thundering waves of thought that batter us repeatedly? Why not try to calm them? Because there is, deep within, a place of silence. There is a place of tranquillity, a place of peace. We need not look for another tranquillity, peace, silence. We already have it. The place where the mind is silent, as the last case taught us. By recognizing and realizing we have this place within us, the wild thoughts will of themselves stop. We need not concern ourselves with them. For our concern gives them power. Not bothering with them depletes their power. One can say, a by-product of zazen is tranquillity and peace of mind. But that is not why we sit. We sit because to sit is the Way. We sit because we are enlightened.

Keizan urges us to turn to the "square inch" of mind we have. That's where everything is. The Unborn. The Light. The Mind.

Should we then not make an effort? Should we be lackadaisical? No and yes. If doing zazen is for a purpose,

Case 22

then it is a waste. There should be effort to sit with determination. We sit to sit, not to become buddhas, not to achieve enlightenment, not to crack a koan.

Then how do we do koan study? We let the koan be. We let the koan seep into our pores as we sit. We circumambulate the koan. One hundred and eight times. We chant it as a mantra. We become one with the koan. There's a story about a monk who was working on the koan, "The Cypress Tree in the Garden." While traveling, he stopped at an inn and was given a room on the ground floor. Later, the innkeeper went out to fetch some wood. He happened to look in the window of the Zen monk and, to his astonishment, saw a cypress tree in the middle of the room. The cypress tree was the monk doing zazen.

Poem

Vasubandu

No way is enough.
Enough for the heavens.
Enough for a cup of coffee.
Enough for no way.
No way for no way.

CASE 23

Manorata

The twenty-second ancestor was the Venerable Manorata. He asked Vasubandhu, "What is the bodhi of all the Buddhas?" The Venerable Vasubandhu said, "It is the original nature of Mind." The master again asked, "What is the original nature of Mind?" The Venerable Vasubandhu said, "It is the emptiness of the six sense bases, the six objects, and the six kinds of consciousness." Hearing this, the master was awakened.

Keizan's Verse
The spirit of shunyata is neither inside nor outside;
Seeing, hearing, forms, and sounds are all empty.

Thoughts

This case concerns itself with the original nature of Mind. What is it? The answer is that it is the emptiness of the six sense bases, the six objects, and the six kinds of consciousness.

Case 23

What does this mean? How could our senses be empty? What is emptiness? What is shunyata? Are we saying that when we hear something we are really not hearing something? Are we saying Johann Sebastian Bach's Chromatic Fantasy and Fugue does not exist? We put the CD in the player, turn it on, and listen. Are we not hearing something? Is that not a harpsichord? Is that not Wanda Landowska playing? We obviously are hearing, and we can distinguish this piece from, say, Mozart's *Marriage of Figaro*. One is a piece written for the harpsichord, while the other is an opera, written for an orchestra and singers. So what does "emptiness of the six sense bases" mean? What does emptiness of the ear mean?

Looking at this deeper, we ask another question. What is it that "hears"? Is it the ear that hears the Chromatic Fantasy and Fugue? It obviously can't be the ear, otherwise a dead person with a perfectly good ear would hear. So we have another question. Where do we hear? The brain? The liver? The big toe of the right foot? Where does the hearing of the Chromatic Fantasy and Fugue take place? A very simple answer, of course, is that it takes place in the Mind. Well, where is the Mind? Hui-k'o, the disciple of Bodhidharma, looked and looked for Mind and couldn't find it anywhere!

The teaching of previous and later cases is that the Mind is empty. Does this mean there is nothing in Mind? If there is nothing, how can we hear Bach's Chromatic Fantasy and Fugue in the Mind? Does emptiness really mean emptiness? I think we can also look at it in another way. I understand that the Chinese ideogram for "emptiness" is the same as the ideogram for "sky." The sky that is full and yet empty. The sky is empty and yet it contains flowers, birds, trees, clouds, thunderstorms, mountaintops—everything in the universe is in the sky—and at the same time the sky itself is empty.

I think this approaches an understanding of what Mind is and what the emptiness of Mind is about. Empty yet full, complete. Everything is within that emptiness. The Chromatic Fantasy and Fugue as well as *The Marriage of Figaro*—all the music that has ever been written and will be written in the future—is in Mind. All the literature that has been written and will be written is in Mind. The emptiness of Mind contains all things.

Poem

Manorata

Sitting on a pillow,
the universe passed by.

It made a rumbling noise
in my stomach.

CASE 24

Haklenayasha

The twenty-third ancestor was the Venerable Haklenayasha. Once the Venerable Manorata said, "I have the unexcelled great Dharma Treasure. You must hear it, accept it, and teach it in the future." Hearing this, the master experienced awakening.

Keizan's Verse
*A white precipice—snow of a great peak
   sticking through the clouds.
Its purity annihilates all details and contrasts
   with the blue sky.*

Thoughts

This case speaks about teaching and the Dharma Treasure. Often I tell students it is easy to be a Zen teacher because there's nothing to teach. And so I am a Zen teacher and, being one, I do not teach. One can also say, the great Dharma Treasure is no treasure. Throughout the *Denkoroku*, Keizan repeatedly turns to the Light and describes it in many ways. Looks at it from many points of view. He is

Haklenayasha

looking at it in this case from the point of view of the Dharma Treasure. Or, the great teaching.

We get a clue when we listen to Shakyamuni's words in the last sermon he gave. He said, "I have been with you for forty years and I have never opened my mouth. I have never taught anything." How can this be? We know Shakyamuni Buddha gave us teachings such as the Four Noble Truths, in which he spoke about *dukkha*, or suffering or anguish, the causes of *dukkha*, the arising of *dukkha*, the termination of *dukkha*, and the way of achieving this termination through the Eightfold Path. He taught the Eightfold Path. But did he teach anything?

In interviewing students, Socrates showed that everything was a process of remembering what they already had within them. If we have it already, what is there to teach? "Look within," says the Buddha, and you will find that you are Buddha.

During one of his travels the Buddha arrived at a village and the villagers said to him, "Look here now, there have been many teachers coming through our village. One teacher says that this and this and so and so is the truth. Another teacher says something completely different, that the truth is so and so, and so and so. A third teacher contradicts the first two and says that the truth is so and so, and so and so. What is the true teaching? What is this great unexcelled treasure? The Buddha's response was "Look inside yourselves and that which you know to be a good thing to do, do, and that which you know not to be a good thing to do, don't do."

Atta Dipa. Be a refuge unto yourselves. Do not rely

Case 24

on others. Do not rely on anything other than yourselves.

Why can't we believe this? Why do we doubt what we already have? Why do we look for something more? For something different? For something else? For something outside ourselves? Why do we think what somebody else has to offer is more important than what we have? Why do we think the words of others are more meaningful than ours?

Zazen takes us to that place within, which illuminates, enlightens, and guides us. All we need to do is sit and turn inside. Click the button of our treasure and allow the illumination of the Light to warm our entire being.

Poem

Haklenayasha

The greatness
of the Dharma Treasure
is that there is no Treasure
and no Dharma

CASE 25

Simhabodhi

The twenty-fourth ancestor was the Venerable Simhabodhi. He asked the twenty-third ancestor, "I want to seek the Way. What concerns should I have?" The ancestor said, "If you want to seek the Way, there is nothing to be concerned about." The master said, "If I have no concerns, who carries out the Buddha activities?" The ancestor said, "If you have some business, these are not merits. If you do nothing, this is Buddha activity. A scripture says, 'The merits I have achieved are not mine.'" Hearing these words, the master entered the wisdom of the Buddhas.

Keizan's Verse
If you want to reveal the sky, do not cover it up. It is empty, tranquil and originally bright.

Thoughts

More on the Way. This case expresses the teaching that the Buddha Way is not a way to walk on. It is not a way we can create. The Way is not something we can make happen.

Case 25

Plainly, Simhabodhi is asking, "What must I do to walk the Way?" "Nothing," says his teacher, Haklenayasha, "there's nothing to be done—just get out of the way and you're there."

The poem that is chanted in Soto Zen monasteries daily, written by Sekito Kisen, "The Identity of Relative and Absolute," has the lines "When you walk the Way you draw no nearer, progress no farther." Sekito teaches that we cannot walk the Way. The Zen practice we do is not the Way. We do Zen practice, period! We are constantly in the way of the Way. Should we remove ourselves? Should we remove our thoughts, our opinions, our beliefs to achieve the Way? Do nothing? How difficult it is to do nothing. Oscar Wilde says, "To do nothing is the most difficult thing in the world. The most difficult and the most intellectual!" We feel we must do something to make *it* happen. Yet whatever we do misses the point. Whatever we do creates an obstacle, because whatever we do we do in the realm of duality. The realm of duality does not contain the Way. Stop doing, and be. Stop thinking about it. Stop planning. Stop creating. Just be. Then, it is possible to be the Way even in duality. If we are working in the kitchen and a knife slips and we cut our hand, we don't stop and think and observe, "Oh, I've cut my hand. Blood is coming out of my hand. I can get an infection. I guess I'd better go to the bathroom, stop the bleeding, put some iodine on the cut, and cover it up with a Band-Aid." What nonsense! When we cut our hand we immediately grab it, go to the bathroom, wash the wound, pour iodine on it, bandage it. All without thought. All without premeditation. We immediately act.

Simhabodhi

Our efforts to achieve the Way are like building a city on top of an already existing city. There is a city within our hearts. What need have we to create another? What need is there to build another building on top of an already existing building? There is a mansion with many rooms within our hearts. We should enter our mansion and abide there. The work has already been done. No need to redo it, for to do it again is extra, and is crazy. All our efforts are toward building a second house. Imagine trying to build a second head and putting it on top of the head we already have? That's nuts! The head we have already works. It has a mouth, nose, ears, eyes, tongue, hair. We can see, taste, smell, hear. What need is there for a second head? It's nuts to try to build a second head. Not only is it nuts, we simply can't do it. All of our ingenuity, all the wisdom which humanity has attained, is unable to make another head. We cannot even make a single hair!

Poem

Simhabodhi

(Do not build a city
on top of another.)

The Way is not a way
of doing or undoing.

Get out of the way
and you are there.

Case 26

Bashashita

The twenty-fifth ancestor was the Venerable Bashashita. The twenty-fourth ancestor said, "I now transmit the Tathagata's Treasure of the Eye of the True Dharma to you. You must guard it and benefit all in the future." The master uncovered the karmic causes of previous lives and received the Mind seal.

Keizan's Verse
At the time blooming flowers and falling leaves are displayed at once,
The king of medicine trees still has no distinct flavor.

Thoughts

The key words in this case are "The master uncovered the karmic causes of previous lives." I believe this is a koan of OneBody. When we speak of OneBody, we speak of all creation being somehow OneBody, somehow connected in ways we do not understand. There are definite links between people. Empathy is proof that this is so. Empathy is the ability to feel the pain of another even though oneself is not in pain, and ability to feel the joy of another even

Bashashita

though we may not have anything personally to be joyful about.

Another of the metaphors of OneBody is the present body we have. The different parts of our body have very specialized functions and tasks. The eye sees, the nose smells, the ear hears, et cetera. Going deeper, the various parts of our nervous system have very highly developed tasks—all of which makes our body work.

Each body part is distinct and complete in itself. Yet they all connect. The foot is not jealous if the hand receives a donut. The hand is not jealous if the foot receives a relaxing footrub. The right hand is not jealous if the left hand receives a donut. The nose is not jealous if the mouth eats a donut. They all connect. Even the foot enjoys the donut, just as the nose enjoys the rub the foot receives. So we see in our own bodies that different body parts create OneBody. So it is with all sentient beings. We are in some way OneBody.

This koan takes OneBody further. It takes it beyond birth and death. To the past and into the future. It says, all bodies that ever existed in the past and will exist in the future are OneBody. This includes Julius Caesar, Cleopatra, Johann Sebastian Bach, the body I presently have, and bodies that are to come after me.

OneBody transcends time and space.

Case 26

Poem

Bashashita I

*Original lightmind
changes faces with time
and the jewel is held
from life to life.*

Bashashita II

*Every breath
a face*

*Every breath
a jewel*

*Every breath
a life*

*Every breath
a death*

Every breath

CASE 27

Punyamitra

The twenty-sixth ancestor was the Venerable Punyamitra. When he was a crown prince, the twenty-fifth ancestor asked him, "You wish to make your home-departure. What thing must you do?" The master replied, "When I make my home-departure, I will not do any particular thing." The ancestor asked, "What thing will you not do?" The master answered, "I will not do any ordinary thing." The ancestor asked, "What thing must you do?" The master answered, "I must do Buddha work." The ancestor said, "The crown prince's wisdom is naturally excellent; you must be a successor of various sages." Then, the ancestor permitted him to make his home-departure.

Keizan's Verse
The original realm is ordinary, without an
   inch of grass;
Where is there room here for the ways of
   Zen?

Case 27

Thoughts

Keizan defines Punyamitra's answers in the following way. He says that "thing" means ordinary things. A thing is not one's own or another's. "Being able to clarify the original mind" is what is called "Buddha work." Keizan also says "original mind" includes all things, and all beings contain original mind. Therefore, there is no difference between monk, layperson, man, woman, Zen teacher, pope, president, congressperson, judge, prisoner, correctional officer—all beings contain original mind. Whatever form of life we have is the Way. We can practice the Way wherever we are. Whatever we do is the expression of the Way. There is no need to go anywhere special to learn teachings, to study special books. Where we are right now is the Way. All we need to do is do it.

Poem

Punyamitra

Space
No inside no outside

Mind
No inside no outside

No monk no layperson

good evil
samsara nirvana

male female
self other

Punyamitra

buddha bum

delusionenlightenment
onetwo

Bright moon
Hot sun

Owwwwwwwww!
Pain in the legs

Case 28

Prajñadhara

The twenty-seventh ancestor was the Venerable Prajñadhara. Once, the twenty-sixth ancestor asked, "Do you remember the past?" The master replied, "I remember being with the master eons ago. The master propounded the great wisdom maha-prajna and I recited the profound sutra. The present event of our meeting probably is connected with that ancient cause."

Keizan's Verse
Moonlight reflected in the bottom of the pond
  is bright in the sky;
The water reaching to the sky is totally clear
  and pure.
Though you scoop it up repeatedly and try to
  know it,
Vast, clarifying all, it remains unknown.

Thoughts

This case is similar to Case 27, Punyamitra, in that it deals with time. In his *teisho*, Keizan says, "To see today is to see eternity. If you look back to eternity, you observe today. . . .

Prajñadhara

When you can reach this realm, it is not past, present, or future, nor is it a matter of sense faculties, objects, and consciousness. Therefore it is said, Dharma succession transcends the three times and realization and experience pervade past and present."

The present moment contains all. *

Poem

Prajñadhara

Wow!
I can feel
the masters
of the Lineage
dance the Lindy Hop
in my heart.

One! Two! Step!
One! Two! Step!

---

*A similar expression of this can be found in the "Burnt Norton" section of T. S. Eliot's masterful "Four Quartets."

CASE 29

Bodhidharma

The twenty-eighth ancestor was the Venerable Bodhidharma. Once the twenty-seventh ancestor, the Venerable Prajñadhara, asked, "What among all things is formless?" The master replied, "Non-arising is formless." The ancestor asked, "What among all things is the greatest?" The master replied, "The true nature of things is the greatest."

Keizan's Verse
There is no distinction or location, no edge or outside.
How could anything be larger than an autumn hair?

Thoughts

The heart of this case is reality. Prajñadhara plumbs Bodhidharma's understanding of reality by asking two questions: "What among all things is formless?" and "What among all things is the greatest?" Bodhidharma's answer to the first question is "Non-arising" or "Non-origination" is formless. His response to the second question is

Bodhidharma

"The true nature of things, or the nature of reality, is the greatest."

Keizan's poem says there is no distinction or location or edge—no outside. Cook's second line of the poem reads, "Could anything be larger than an autumn hair?" Cleary's translation is "Is there anything at all even in the slightest?"

Put all this together and you have reality. Non-arising or non-origination. The true nature of things, that for which there is no distinction or location. No inside. No outside. No bounds. An autumn hair blowing in the wind. The Hua Yen scriptures tell us the entire universe is in the tip of a hair. Reality is the now, the blowing of the wind, the movement of the leaves at the tips of trees, the singing of the birds, dawn zazen, the flowing of the stream. We know reality in our bones.

Poem

Bodhidharma

Dawn zazen.
A cold winter morning.
The wind blows
through walls and leaky windows,
chilling my bones.

Well, here's to the old
gap-toothed one!

Case 30

Hui-k'o

The twenty-ninth ancestor, China's second ancestor, great master Hui-k'o, studied with the twenty-eighth ancestor and served him. One day he said to the ancestor, "I have already put an end to all conditions." The ancestor asked, "Doesn't that result in death?" The master replied, "It does not result in death." "What is your proof?" asked the ancestor. "I am always clearly aware. Therefore, words are inadequate," said the master. The ancestor said, "This is the Mind-substance realized by all Buddhas. Have no doubt."

Keizan's Verse
In the realm that is empty and bright,
   conditions and thought are exhausted;
It is clear, alert, and always bright.

Thoughts

This is a special case. Hui-k'o was the first Chinese ancestor. He received the Light from Bodhidharma, who was Indian. Now it would illuminate China. In the same way, Dogen

Hui-k'o

was the transmission vehicle of the Light from China to Japan.

Metaphors of Light are all around Hui-k'o. For instance, his parents were unable to have children until one night they saw a strange light in the room; thereupon Hui-k'o's mother became pregnant. Later, he was named Kuang, which means "light," because of the illuminated room.

Hui-k'o became a very learned man. He studied all the Buddhist books as well as the teachings of Lao-tzu, Confucius, Chuang-tzu, and the *I Ching*. One day while sitting in meditation, zazen, he saw a spirit in the form of a light that appeared to him. It advised him to go south. He realized that Light was spiritual and so he changed his name to Shen-kuang, which means "Spiritual Light." After he was accepted by Bodhidharma, he changed his name to Hui-k'o, which means "potential for Dharma."

After becoming Bodhidharma's student, he continued to live and work with Bodhidharma for eight years, until Bodhidharma died. Hui-k'o passed on the Dharma to Seng-ts'an and went to practice on his own. He removed his robes and worked with the poor. He worked in the streets and marketplaces with butchers and cleaners of toilets—with the lowest of the low—the outcasts. In this way, Keizan says, he concealed his Light and obliterated all traces of his status. So he lived a layman's life for the next thirty years. Finally, because of the jealousy of another priest, he was falsely accused, and executed on the sixteenth day in the third month in A.D. 593.

What did Bodhidharma teach Hui-k'o? Keizan says

Case 30

he didn't teach him anything in particular. His major teaching is in one sentence:

When you put an end to all external conditions,
and there is no grasping of the mind internally,
and the mind becomes like a wall,
then you will enter the Way.

Another tradition says Bodhidharma's teaching is in the Lankavatara Sutra and the teaching he transmitted to Hui-k'o was this sutra. The Lankavatara Sutra was studied in all Zen monasteries during the early years of Zen in China.

The other startling legend about Hui-k'o was his determination to study the Way. He was already a very accomplished Buddhist priest and teacher. He excelled in the various religious traditions of the day. Yet he was led to Bodhidharma knowing that Bodhidharma had *It*. The legend says that when he first approached Bodhidharma it was snowing, so he stood outside Bodhidharma's hut in the snow. Bodhidharma wouldn't let him in. Finally, next morning, there was Hui-k'o, hip-deep in snow. Bodhidharma asked him, "What do you want?" "I want to study the Way with you," said Hui-k'o. Bodhidharma rejected him again, saying, "It's too difficult. It takes many years of hard practice to study the Way." This tradition of refusal of applicants takes place today when a Zen monk in Japan goes to a monastery to study. The monk remains outside, in a narrow courtyard, in kneeling position, sometimes for days before he can enter. Always the first response to the applicant's entreaty is, "Go away, there's no room for you." And still the applicant remains waiting and waiting

Hui-k'o

until room is found. Keizan says in his commentary that this type of behavior is part of the teaching.

Hui-k'o, the legend continues, went so far to show his determination to study the Way that he cut off his arm and presented it to Bodhidharma. Seeing this fantastic, crazy mutilation, Bodhidharma was finally convinced of Hui-k'o's sincerity to practice and accepted him as his student.

What can one say of this? Do we feel today that practice is a matter of life and death? How many of us practice as if our lives depended upon it?

In my own case, I came to Zen practice because I met two old friends of mine with whom I grew up in Brooklyn. The reunion was wonderful. We had a great time remembering the old days in the streets of Brooklyn—our gangs, our fights, selling pretzels on street corners, going to Catholic school, roller-skating on the streets, making roller-scooters out of wooden vegetable boxes, playing baseball on the corner lot. The following week, both of these friends died of heart attacks. This startled me. I realized that one of them could have been me. So I looked at my life. Then the question arose, "What would I do if this was the last day of my life?" So, I turned to Zen practice, which was something I had been hovering over for many years. Then, there certainly was a sense of urgency in my practice. As the years go by and I don't die, the sense of urgency slips.

I read somewhere that a Catholic saint was asked how to pray and the saint replied, "Begin each prayer with the knowledge that you will die before you finish your prayer." That's really powerful stuff! Do we begin each session of

Case 30

zazen with the knowledge that before we rise we may be dead? If we did, how powerful would our zazen be? Many Zen masters have said Zen practice is a matter of life and death. The fact of life and death was the turning point in the life of Shakyamuni. Dogen advises us to sit as if we were extinguishing a fire on top of our heads. That's the level of determination to put to our zazen.

The interesting thing about Hui-k'o's case is that nothing is really transmitted. He is simply told to empty his mind. Upon hearing this, Hui-k'o says, "I have already put an end to everything." Bodhidharma asked, "Doesn't this result in death?" "No," Hui-k'o says. "Why not?" And Hui-k'o's thundering response is "I am always clearly aware!" Very important words. Always aware! Always there! Always awake! Always present! Always alert! The Light within transmits! And the Light is always shining. Hui-k'o is always present in the Light. Therefore, there is no need for words. There is no need for teachings. Therefore, there is unity. There is no separation between subject and object. There is just Light. Light.

Hui-k'o is a full and resplendent manifestation of Light.

Poem

Hui-k'o

Standing in the snow—
No arm to offer—
Not even a fingernail—

CASE 31

Seng-ts'an

The thirtieth ancestor, China's third ancestor, was great master Seng-ts'an. He visited the twenty-ninth ancestor and said, "My body is infected with leprosy. I beg you, O priest, to cleanse me of my wrongdoing." The ancestor said, "Bring me your wrongdoing and I will cleanse you." The master paused awhile and then said, "When I look for my wrongdoing, I cannot find it." The ancestor replied, "I have already cleansed you of your wrongdoing. You must rely on the Buddha, Dharma, and the Community of believers."

Keizan's Verse
Empty of essential nature, without inside or outside,
Good and bad leave no traces.
Mind and Buddha are fundamentally the same,
And Dharma and Community can be understood in the same way.

Case 31

Thoughts

Seng-ts'an is the author of the wonderful poem "On Trust in the Heart." Both of the groups I work with, The Dragon Gate Sangha, at the Eastern Correctional Institute at Napanoch, New York, and the White Cliff Sangha, a group in New Paltz, New York, regularly chant this sutra. We include it in our *Book of Zen Sutras*.

This koan is about karmic illness. It implies that illness is the result of karmic acts in the past. Seng-ts'an had leprosy and was therefore guilty of a wrongdoing. The case does not specifically say the wrongdoing took place in the past or in a past life. Seng-ts'an said, "When I look for my wrongdoing, I cannot find it." This can mean it is not a wrongdoing Seng-ts'an committed in this lifetime, and so the wrongdoing must be karmic.

However, there could be another interpretation. This discussion is similar to the *mondo* (a term that means, a question and answer or discussion between teacher and disciple, leading to insight) between Bodhidharma and Hui-k'o. Hui-k'o told Bodhidharma, "My mind is going crazy. It is full of thoughts and activities. Please help me settle my troubled mind." Bodhidharma said, "Bring me your mind and I will put it to rest." Hui-k'o sat with Bodhidharma's response, probably for weeks, maybe even months, maybe even years. The question he grappled with may have been, "How can I bring my mind to him? How can I show him my mind? How can I present my mind?"

Then one asks, "What is mind?"

In another interview, Hui-k'o probably just sat before Bodhidharma, silent and dumb, with nothing to say, nothing to ask. Just sitting, the two of them. Bodhidharma, sensing the time was ripe, asked Hui-k'o, "Have you brought me your mind?" Hui-k'o responded, "I've looked and looked and looked for my mind and I can't find it." Bodhidharma then said, "You see, I have already settled your mind for you."

As we can see, there is a similar situation in Case 31 between Seng-ts'an and Hui-k'o. Only in this case, Seng-ts'an speaks of wrongdoing. Why can't he find his wrongdoing? Is he saying he is a saint? Is he saying there is no connection between his acts and his illness? Has he gone beyond morality? Beyond labeling acts as right or wrong? Is he simply describing acts as they are?

We are experts at morality. We put moral labels on the nuttiest things. It is "good" to get up early in the morning. It is "bad" to get up late in the morning. I had a "good" walk today. I had a "bad" walk today. This was a "good" zazen for me. This was a "bad" zazen for me.

My daughter, Cellina, and I were talking about this recently in connection with her two-week-old baby girl, Michelle Monet. We were talking about education, and the bringing up of the baby, and the many wonderful things Cellina and her child have to look forward to. We were talking about how children immediately begin to pick up our crazy morality, and get corrupted and screwed up by what we mistakenly pass off as education. One of the problems is our crazy "good" and "bad" labels. We inflict or, rather, infect, the child with our nonsense-morality and

Case 31

our crazy karma. For instance, as we were riding in the car, we found ourselves saying how "good" Michelle is to have slept during our ride rather than cry. By saying she was "good" for sleeping we are saying sleep is good and crying is bad. What nonsense! Later, during the drive, Michelle did cry. So, Cellina found a convenient place to stop and park the car. She went to the backseat, took Michelle out of her car-crib, and fed her.

When Michelle sleeps she sleeps, and when Michelle cries she cries. There's nothing good or bad about sleeping or crying. Crying is crying. Sleeping is sleeping. One doesn't say, "You bad child," for crying. One stops the car and tries to figure out what is bothering the child. It could be soiled diapers. It could be colic. It could be any number of reasons. In this case, Michelle was hungry. So her mother fed her. No good or bad involved. By eliminating the words "good" and "bad," we directly deal with the child, with reality, and do not burden and infect the child with our screwed-up morality.

It seems to me Seng-ts'an has seen the meaning behind Hui-k'o's words "Bring me your wrongdoing and I will cleanse you." In his meditation, he sees that the idea of wrongdoing is a moral label. It is a delusion. We cannot find wrongdoing. There is doing. Not *wrong*doing or *good*doing. There is just doing. Doing. Having seen this, Seng-ts'an is cleansed.

Being a leper is not good or bad. It is being a leper. A leper dealing with his or her leprosy as an illness. Being infected with any illness does not mean it is good or bad. Simply deal with the illness. Take the aspirin. Call the doctor in

Seng-ts'an

the morning. Do your lower-back exercises. Put that cold that turns into a fever to bed. Deal with the high fever. We take appropriate medicines, drink hot tea with lemon. Whatever. We deal with it as it is, without any labels. Without saying, "What did I do to deserve this?" We have it. We deal with it. *Basta!*

I can think of no better way to end these thoughts than a line from Seng-ts'an's poem "On Trust in the Heart":

No blame, no Dharmas; no arising, no thought.

Poem

Seng-ts'an

I used to get headaches
all the time.

Now I watch the dance
of the clouds
in the wind.

They spin and toss,
like thoughts.

Sometimes,
they even sigh.

CASE 32

Tao-hsin

The thirty-first ancestor, China's fourth ancestor, Zen master Tao-hsin, bowed to the great master Seng-ts'an, and said, "I beg the priest in his great compassion to give me the teaching of liberation." The ancestor replied, "Who is binding you?" The master said, "No one is binding me." The ancestor answered, "Then why are you seeking liberation?" With these words, the master was greatly awakened.

Keizan's Verse

Mind is empty, and pure knowing contains no right or wrong.
In this, what is there to be bound or liberated?
Even though it becomes the four great elements and five skandhas, in the end, seeing, hearing, forms, and sounds are nothing else than Mind.

Tao-hsin

Thoughts

These cases go through cycles and there are similarities and subtle differences between cases. The last three cases are similar. They all refer to the delusions we hang on to that prevent us from seeing and expressing the Way. The major question in this case is "What binds us?" "What trips us up?" As we look deeply into things that bind us, can we find anything? In interviews, some students have told me their minds are full of crazy thoughts, and in perpetual strife; that there are thunderstorms and earthquakes in their minds—tidal waves. I challenge them to bring me these thoughts. They can't do it. It is impossible to hold a thought. The reason is, we are always moving. Holding on to a thought is like holding water in one's hands. There's no way to contain water in our hands. No way to contain a thought in our mind. It will slip through our hands and out of our mind. What is thought? Can you put it on a table and look at it? Can you slice it? Can you weigh it? Measure it in any way? Is it possible that there is no way to contain thoughts because there is no such thing as "thought"? That thoughts are delusions?

What binds us? Our thoughts. So the crazy situation is that something that possibly has no existence is screwing us up. That's nuts! We are our own problem. We need not seek liberation because we are already liberated. We are complete. We are the Light. Our crazy thoughts screw us up. Our thoughts keep us from realizing and expressing the Light. This is nuts!

Case 32

Poem

Tao-hsin

thoughts
twist into knots
trapped

a spider
stuck
in its own web

Case 33

Hung-jen

The thirty-second ancestor, China's fifth ancestor, Zen master Hung-jen, met the thirty-first ancestor on the road to Huang-mei. The ancestor asked him, "What is your family name (hsing)"? The master replied, "I have a nature (hsing) but it is not an ordinary name (hsing)." The ancestor asked, "What is its name?" Replied the master, "It is Buddha-nature (fo-hsing)." The ancestor asked, "Have you no name?" The master answered, "Because Buddha-nature is empty, I have none." The ancestor thought to himself that he was a vessel of the Dharma and transmitted the Dharma and robe to him.

Keizan's Verse
Moon bright, water pure, the autumn sky clear,
how can a speck of cloud mark this immense purity?

Case 33

Thoughts

This koan is about Buddha-nature. Buddha is OneBody. It transcends time and space. How can I speak of Buddha-nature? The image I get in considering this koan is the famous Zen circle one often sees:

The circle is open because there is no inside or outside the circle. This is the circle of OneBody. OneBody transcends time and space. "All Buddhas throughout space and time" is a line from a refrain chanted in Soto Zen service. The complete *gatha* is:

All Buddhas throughout space and time
All Bodhisattvas, Mahasattvas,
Maha, Prajña, Paramita.

It includes all things. We are part of, and somehow connected to, that which at one time we called Hung-jen and Shakyamuni Buddha. There is a connection between us and part of Hui-k'o, Bodhidharma, Mozart, Beethoven, Leonardo da Vinci, Michelangelo, Caesar Borgia, Julius Caesar, Napoleon, Jesus Christ, Judas Iscariot, all the murderers who are sitting in the death rows of the world, waiting for execution, and all of their victims. We are also part of the terrorists of the bombing in Oklahoma City. We are part of the Chinese who are occupying Tibet, raping that poor country. Part of all the combatants in every ongoing war. The judge, jury, and defendant in the O. J. Simpson trial. The victims of that horrendous double murder.

OneBody means all of this. And deeper and more. Not merely "connected." Not merely "a part of." We are! We are all the above—the victims, the executioners, the heroes, heroines, murderers—all of them—without exception. All somehow held together with the mystic glue of our bodies and of Buddha-nature. Of the Light. The Unborn. The Holy Spirit.

Now are we really talking about Buddha-nature? Are we not talking in the same sense that one speaks of the immortal or great soul? What is the difference between Buddha-nature and the soul? If soul is apart from us, it is not Buddha-nature. Buddha-nature is in the very interstices of our cell structure.

How is OneBody possible? Through the emptiness of Buddha-nature. This *gatha* is chanted after every Zen service:

All Buddhas throughout Space and Time,
All Bodhisattvas, Mahasattvas,
Maha, Prajña, Paramita.

All creation exists in emptiness.
Keizan's poem illuminates this dramatically:

Case 33

*Moon bright, water pure, the autumn sky clear,
how can a speck of cloud mark this immense purity?*

Poem

Hung-jen

*clouds
circling the heavens
draw different shapes*

*look
there's the face
I had before
I was born*

*now you see it
now you see it
now you see it*

CASE 34

Hui-neng

The thirty-third ancestor, China's sixth ancestor, was Zen master Hui-neng. He worked in the rice-hulling shed at Huang-mei. Once, Zen master Hung-jen entered the shed and asked, "Is the rice white yet?" The master answered, "It's white, but it hasn't been sifted yet." Hung-jen struck the mortar three times with his staff. The master shook the sifting basket three times and entered the ancestor's room.

Keizan's Verse
Striking the mortar—the sound was loud, echoing beyond time and space;
Sifting the clouds—the silver moon appeared, and the night was deep and clear.

Thoughts

I bow before Hui-neng. Hui-neng, the sixth ancestor, is the person most responsible for Zen as we know it today, who transformed the practice that was Indian in custom and nature and adapted it to his own traditions—the customs and

Case 34

sensitivities and feelings of China. Much has been written, of course, about Hui-neng and there is little I can add. The great mystery of Hui-neng is that there is hardly any historical data about him. The only record is a list of senior students of Hung-jen, the fifth ancestor. Hui-neng's name is one of a dozen or so on this list. Hui-neng, himself, left no writings. There are no direct transcriptions of his teachings contemporary with him. Most of what we know about Hui-neng and the legends, stories, and myths of his life come from his student Shen-hui. There is also not much known about Shen-hui. In the Platform Sutra, attributed to Hui-neng, Shen-hui has a very minor role and is not a chief disciple. It was he, however, who established Hui-neng, and insisted upon the dominance of Hui-neng as the sixth ancestor. At that time there was a conflicting claim made by Shen-hsui, also in that list of disciples of Hung-jen. He was the leader of the Northern School of Zen, and claimed the title of the sixth ancestor. The Southern School of Zen, dominated and survived; therefore, Hui-neng is the sixth ancestor.

One of the major teachings of Hui-neng was his electrifying definition of zazen as being the "non-separation between subject and object." OneBody. He does not say zazen is meditation. In all the writings and teachings attributed to Hui-neng, rarely does he even mention zazen, except in his last sermon where he counsels his followers to meditate. For him, whenever a person becomes one-with, whatever the object, then zazen takes place. Hui-neng took zazen—Zen—out of the meditation hall and monasteries and brought it into everyday life. He took the mystique of

Hui-neng

meditation—zazen—and made it ordinary. Ordinariness is one of the hallmarks of the Zen which Hui-neng taught and practiced.

He was a very ordinary man—in fact, illiterate. He had never read the scriptures, or heard them, or had them read to him. He knew nothing about Zen or Buddhism, and yet upon hearing one verse from the Diamond Sutra, all became clear. At that very moment, he became enlightened. I think the biographies make a great point of his illiteracy to establish the supremacy of the true self over the acquired self. The supremacy of natural, everyday, common-sense knowledge, as opposed to acquired, learned knowledge.

Ananda had to struggle for over forty years to make the Buddha's words his own. Hui-neng's words were always his own, for he had the word from the first moment of his enlightenment. He was always his own person. He knew who he was. He knew he had the Dharma and yet he did not boast about it. He submitted himself and his practice to his teacher. He also stood up to his teacher and did not retreat from what he knew to be so. The meeting between Hung-jen and Hui-neng illustrates this.

Hung-jen asked, "Where do you come from?" "I come from the South." Well, that's tantamount to saying, "I come from Brooklyn." (Can anything good come out of Brooklyn?) "What are you looking for?" asked Hung-jen. "I'm looking for Buddha-nature." "Can one give Buddha-nature to a person from the South, a land of barbarians?" (Can one give Buddha-nature to someone from Brooklyn, a land of thieves, thugs, and barbarians?) Hui-neng snaps

Case 34

right back and says, "Can Buddha-nature be circumscribed by geography?" Is there a north or south to Buddha-nature? I am certain Hung-jen saw in the piercing eyes of Hui-neng that he had it! This person is complete. Yet Hui-neng accepted Hung-jen's order to go and work in the rice-mill.

Hui-neng did so, for the following seven years, deep in the pits of the rice-mill, far away from the zendo, far away from the hub of the monastery, far away from the glories and rituals of the Zen service, and from meditation halls. Knowing all the time he had it; yet he submitted. He waited until his teacher, the fifth ancestor, the person who embodied the Dharma, said, "OK!"

That's what this koan is about—the recognition of Hui-neng by the fifth ancestor.

"Is the rice white yet?" The rice is Hui-neng's spirit. Have all the dirt and dross of the rice—all the impurities of your life been polished off? Are you complete? "Yes, the rice is white, but hasn't been sifted yet." Yes, but recognition has not yet come. I wait for recognition. I await the sifting that only you can give. Thereupon Hung-jen struck the mortar three times with his staff, sifting. In this way, he recognized Hui-neng as the sixth ancestor.

Even after recognition, Hui-neng continued to live an ordinary life. One of the stories is that he joined forces with a group of hunters and became their cook.

One of the great teachings of Hui-neng is to trust the word in one's own heart. To know that is all one needs. Everything one reads or hears is commentary on the word that is within one's heart. Knowing we have it, we learn

Hui-neng

from Hui-neng to wait until our teacher confirms our word. Recognition. Waiting for the authentication of our word. When our word becomes one with the word of our teacher, then we may speak it. This is what transmission is all about. This is what happens in Case 34.

Poem

Hui-neng

the knocking
reverberating
throughout space and time—
scatters my bones

Who's breathing on my face?
Who's whispering in my ears?

Case 35

Ch'ing-yüan

The thirty-fourth ancestor was great master Ch'ing-yüan. He practiced in the community of Ts'ao-ch'i. He asked the sixth ancestor, "What should I do so as not to land in some class or stage?" The ancestor asked, "What have you done so far?" The master replied, "I have not even tried the four holy truths." The ancestor asked, "Into what stage will you end up?" The master said, "If I still have not tried the holy truths, what stage can there be?" The ancestor was greatly impressed with his potential.

Keizan's Verse
When a bird flies, it comes and goes, but there are no traces.
How can you look for stages on the dark path?

Thoughts

This is a case about truth and reality. I'm fortunate to live in the southern Catskill Mountains of New York, in an area called Shawangunk (pronounced "Shongum"). The

Ch'ing-yüan

word means "white stones." Rock climbers from all over the country and the world come to climb the nearby Shawangunk hills (often called the "Gunks"). There are many miles of trails in the Gunks. Not only do I live here, but I have two dogs who need to have a long walk every day. And so it is my privilege to take them on daily walks in the Gunks. One day, as we were walking, all of a sudden I noticed mountain laurel in full bloom all around me. The mountain laurel is a very hardy plant. Its root twists into beautiful patterns that remind me of the California manzanita. I often pick up dried-out old roots and whittle, sand, and polish them for use as *katsus* or service sticks in Soto Zen religious service. The mountain laurel has many buds, and blooms white. Not much aroma. The view of a forest or hillside, covered with mountain laurel just after the buds have popped open, is breathtaking.

The mountain laurel is in the Gunks all year long. It's ubiquitous. One forgets it when it's not in bloom, or when it's covered with snow in winter. Spring is coming. Everything's still bare. It's hard to distinguish mountain laurel from other vegetation. Then when it's in bloom, it's everywhere.

It is here all the time but we don't realize it. So we practice and practice and practice, hoping to advance from one stage to the other. We do koan study, cracking our heads against them, presenting our koans, our understandings. Finally, we pass our koans, go on to the next ones, and it feels as if we are moving from one level to another. The reality, however, is that the mountain laurel is everywhere. The Holy, or Noble, Truths are not something to

Case 35

practice. The Holy Truths are present and ubiquitous. Nothing to practice. "No stages," as Keizan says in his poem, on the "dark path"—on the path of realization. Realization is always here. We may not see it. We may not feel it. But it's here. Someday, one day, in each of our lives it will burst.

Poem

Ch'ing-yüan

ah
the mountain laurel
bursting
like popcorn
all over
the forest

CASE 36

Shih-t'ou

The thirty-fifth ancestor, great master Shih-t'ou, visited Ch'ing-yüan. Ch'ing-yüan asked, "Where are you from?" The master replied, "I come from Ts'ao-ch'i." Ch'ing-yüan then raised his hossu *and asked, "Does this exist at Ts'ao-ch'i?" The master answered, "It's not only nonexistent at Ts'ao-ch'i, but it doesn't exist in India either." Ch'ing-yüan asked him, "You haven't been to India yet, have you?" The master said, "If I went, it would exist." Ch'ing-yüan said, "That's not good enough; say more." The master replied, "Master, you should say half of it and not depend completely on me." Ch'ing-yüan said, "I don't refuse to speak to you, but I am afraid that after this, no one will be deeply awakened." The master said, "It's not that it will not exist, it's just that no one will be able to express it." Ch'ing-yüan hit him with the* hossu *and the master was greatly awakened.*

Case 36

Keizan's Verse

With one raising of the hossu, *he held up the totality of the Way;*
Never by so much as a hair did Shih-t'ou ever deviate from it.

Thoughts

The key to this case is the word "this." "Does 'this' exist at Ts'ao-ch'i?" What is "this"? Is "this" the *hossu*? (The *hossu* is a ceremonial fly-whisk used by Zen masters as a sign of their possession of the Dharma.) Is it the *hossu*? Is it the Dharma? Is it the Zen master himself? What is "this" that doesn't exist in India? It doesn't exist at Ts'ao-ch'i (which is where Hui-neng is). Where does it exist if not in these places? What does Shih-t'ou mean when he says, "If I went to India it would exist." Why does his teacher say, "That's not good enough, say more"? This is similar to the koan "What do you do when you meet the Buddha on the road?" You kill him! When one understands the reasons for killing the Buddha, one understands why "this" does not exist in India, or in China or in Africa, or in New York City or in Los Angeles. If it doesn't exist in those places, where does it exist? And what is "this" that doesn't exist anyplace?

Poem

Shih-t'ou

like a blind turtle
swimming on the sea of changes
coming and going
up and down
around and around

Case 37

Yüeh-shan

The thirty-sixth ancestor, great master Yüeh-shan, visited Shih-t'ou and asked him, "I understand the twelve-part teachings of the three vehicles, for the most part, but I hear that in the South they directly point to the human mind, see their natures, and become Buddhas. This is still not clear to me. I humbly ask you in your compassion to explain it." The ancestor said, "This way won't do and not this way won't do, and both this way and not this way won't do. How about you?" The master was speechless. The ancestor said, "Your conditions for understanding are not here. You should go to great master Ma." Accordingly, the master went and paid his respects to Ma-tsu and asked the same question. The ancestor said, "Sometimes I make Him raise his eyebrows and blink, sometimes I do not make Him raise his eyebrows and blink. Sometimes raising the eyebrows and blinking is all right, sometimes raising the eyebrows and blinking is not all right. How about you?" With these words, the master was greatly awakened and he bowed. The ancestor asked, "What truth have you seen that makes you bow?"

Yüeh-shan

The master replied, "When I was with Shih-t'ou, it was like a mosquito mounting an iron ox." The ancestor said, "Since you are so, you must guard it well, but still, your master is Shih-t'ou."

Keizan's Verse
That One whose whole life is extremely active and lively
We call the One who raises the eyebrows and blinks.

Thoughts

The Zen masters say there are two types of power: *joriki*, or self power, and *toriki*, or other power. Calling upon Avalokiteshvara either in the form of the powerful chant *Enmei Jukku Kannon Gyo* or by the equally powerful *mantra* of Tara, *Om Tare Tuttare Ture Svaha*, or by the other powerful mantra *Om Mani Padme Hum*, or by invoking the name of the Buddha, *Namu Amida Butsu*—all this is *toriki*. Calling on the power of the universe. Getting into tune with the power of universe. Getting in alignment with the power of the universe—such is *toriki*.

Joriki is seeking within. Going deep until one arrives at "this!" Until one sees and knows that which blinks the eye and that which does not blink the eye. This is *joriki*. Becoming one with all things. All things one.

I say there's another power. One can call this no-power. *No-riki*. Or *mu*. Or powerlessness. One speaks of the great fire that one has no way to enter into, or the clear blue lake that one can approach from any place on its

135

shoreline. The heart of the fire and the heart of the lake are the same. Once we burst through the roaring flames, there are no flames. Once we dive deep into the lake, there is no water.

So it is with the Way. A dialogue Shih-t'ou had with Yüeh-shan is very important. Yüeh-shan was meditating. Shih-t'ou asked him, "What are you doing?" Yüeh-shan: "I'm not doing anything." Shih-t'ou: "If you're not doing anything, what a waste of time it is." Yüeh-shan: "If I were wasting my time, I'd be doing something."

Zazen is the nonact of not doing anything. There is no seeking in zazen. There is no discovery. There is no goal. There are no steps. No achievements. Counting the breaths is a hindrance. When the time comes, one puts away the counting of the breaths and turns to *shikantaza*—just sitting. Then there is just *this*.

This really rubs against our nature. We want to do that which is meaningful. We don't want to waste our time. We want to be doing something. We want to be on the Way. That's why it's difficult to do zazen. There is no "way" to do zazen. That's why Dogen taught *shikantaza*. Just sitting. No thoughts. Non-thinking. Think nonthinking.

Ma-tsu asks Yüeh-shan, "What did you realize that makes you bow?" Yüeh-shan replied, "When I was with Shih-t'ou, I was like a mosquito trying to bite an iron ox." Become the mosquito. What can a mosquito do to an iron ox? No way to penetrate. Each attempt at penetration blunts our fangs. No matter how sharp our bite, we break our teeth. Sit until your teeth bleed. Penetrate the impenetrable. Penetrate penetration. Sit, therefore, without effort.

Yüeh-shan

Can we accept this? Can we accept the zazen that has nothing in it? Can we accept jumping from the hundred-foot pole? Into what? The abyss? That would be easy. The conundrum of the hundred-foot pole koan is that there is no pole. There is no place to jump to or from. This koan reveals our delusions, our attachments.

Poem

Yüeh-shan

the way
neither marked
nor unmarked
high low
here there
this that
not this not that
not the great blue pool
not the giant ball of fire

not Dante's dark wood
not Dorothy's yellow road

leads nowhere

useless

why bother

Case 38

Yün-yen

The thirty-seventh ancestor was great master Yün-yen. He studied at first with Pai-chang for twenty years and afterward he studied with Yüeh-shan. Yüeh-shan asked him, "What dharma does Pai-chang teach?" The master said, "Once, he entered the hall to speak and all the monks were standing in rows. He suddenly scattered them with his staff. Then, he called out, 'O monks!' When they turned around, Pai-chang asked, 'What is it?' Yüeh-shan said, 'Why didn't you say that before? Today, thanks to you, I have been able to meet brother Pai-chang.' " With these words, the master was greatly awakened.

Keizan's Verse

A solitary boat proceeds unaided in the bright
   moonlight;
If you turn around and look, the reeds on the
   ancient shore do not sway.

Yün-yen

Thoughts

In his commentary on this koan, Keizan says the basic point of studying Zen and learning the Way is to clarify mind and awaken to the essentials. Yün-yen had studied with Pai-chang for twenty years and still didn't get it. It's possible to study and practice Zen, going through all the motions, learning all the words, all the sutras, and still not have it.

Recently, a Zen student told me a story. She had gone through deep emotional turmoil. She turned to a senior Zen student she had known for many years and shared her distress with him. To her amazement, whenever she would see him again, not once did he ask how she was doing. She could not understand this. How could someone so advanced in Zen practice have so little feeling, be so lacking in compassion, never to inquire? Not once, thereafter, did he ask, "How are you doing?" I think this is another case of somebody who had practiced Zen for many years, like Yün-yen, and still did not get it.

That's why Zen teachers go through all sorts of "expedient means" to prod their students to find it. To clarify their minds. To understand and find their true selves. Sometimes the tactics Zen teachers use may be bizarre, but always they try to get students to jump over their ruts of tranquillity and habitual patterns to find it.

So it is in this case. Pai-chang tried to get his students to find it. He was making no headway, so he dismissed them and as they were leaving, he shouted after them, "Hey! Monks!" When they turned around: "What is it?"

Case 38

Still they didn't get it. Not even Yün-yen got it. Only afterwards, when he was describing the situation to Yüeh-shan did he realize what was happening.

One can attach to anything. I think the worst attachments are the best things. Oscar Wilde said, "The worst thing about a bad system is the good in it." The goodness perpetuates the bad system. So it is with Zen practice. Whatever achievements we get to, we need to drop. Whatever we learn, we need to get rid of. Emptiness is all. Always empty the cup. Even emptiness itself can be an attachment. Emptiness does not mean not having. Emptiness means being poised for action. Being ready. Being ripe. Being open. In that state—it's almost an isometric state—it's possible to catch a glimpse of it. It's possible to respond to Pai-chang's question, "What is it?"

Poem

Yün-yen

volley
ping . . . pong
till your opponent's
off center
and the ball is right
then

> *slam!!!*

CASE 39

Tung-shan

The thirty-eighth ancestor was great master Tung-shan. He visited Yün-yen and asked, "Who can hear the nonsentient preach the Dharma?' Yün-yen answered, "The nonsentient can hear the nonsentient preach the Dharma." The master asked, "Do you hear it?" Yün-yen replied, "If I could hear it, you would not be able to hear me preach the Dharma." The master said, "In that case, Tung-shan does not hear you preach the Dharma." Yün-yen said, "If you still don't hear me preach the Dharma, how much less can you hear the nonsentient preach the Dharma?" The master was greatly awakened at this point and he spoke this verse:

Wonderful! Wonderful!
The preaching of the Dharma by the
   nonsentient is inconceivable.
If you try to hear with your ears, it is hard to
   understand;
When you listen with your mind's eye, then
   you know it.

Yün-yen approved.

Case 39

Keizan's Verse

Extremely fine subtle consciousness is not emotional attachment;
It constantly makes That One preach keenly.

Thoughts

There are two meanings to the Sanskrit word "dharma." With a capital "D" the word means the teaching of the Buddha. With a small "d" the word means phenomena. Therefore, all phenomena are teachers. Every bird, tree, blade of grass, animal, cat, dog, frog, ant, cockroach, spider—every flower, and chairs, tables, rugs, windows, gardens, garages, rocking chairs, walking sticks, flowing streams, bridges, mountains, lakes, oceans, clouds, sky—all phenomena are teachers. All phenomena are the Buddha, teaching. This case specifically points to this fact.

The question Tung-shan asks is "How can one hear the teaching of the inanimate?" Who can hear the teaching of a running brook or of a mountain? Again we come to the great metaphor of the *Denkoroku*—Light. We stand in the Light. We place ourselves in the Light. Then it is possible to hear the teachings of a mountain and of a running brook. It's as simple as that. It is not something we bring words to, nor do we use words to explicate that which is being taught by the brook. We just walk by the brook. Walk with the brook. Walk in the brook. Splash ourselves with the water of the brook. Become the brook. Become the mountain.

Poem

Tung-shan

*Listen with your heart
to the wind blowing
through the trees.
Are the leaves chanting sutras?*

*Listen to the beat
of the fishdrum branches
beating time against their trunks.*

Listen to the Ino-*Spruce lead the chant
and all Buddhas throughout space and time
join in.*

*No Bach cantata surpasses—
no Monteverdi canon equals—
no Gregorian chant matches—
the song of the singing trees.*

CASE 40

Yun-chu

The thirty-ninth ancestor was great master Yun-chu. He studied with Tung-shan. Tung-shan asked him, "What is your name?" The master replied, "Yun-chu." Tung-shan said, "Say it from beyond." The master said, "If I speak from beyond, I cannot say that I am Yun-chu." Tung-shan said, "That is the same answer I gave when I was with Yün-yen."

Keizan's Verse
Never has it been bound to names and forms;
How can you speak of it as "beyond" or
    "relative"?

Thoughts

This koan deals with the problem of names. Let me turn to Shakespeare. In *Romeo and Juliet,* act 2, scene 2, lines 33 and following.

JULIET: O Romeo, Romeo! wherefore art thou Romeo?
Deny thy father and refuse thy name:
Or, if thou wilt not, be but sworn my love,
And I'll no longer be a Capulet.

ROMEO: *[Aside] Shall I hear more, or shall I speak at this?*

JULIET: *'Tis but thy name that is my enemy;*
Thou art thyself, though not a Montague.
What's Montague? It is nor hand, nor foot,
Nor arm, nor face, nor any other part
Belonging to a man. O, be some other name!
What's in a name? That which we call a rose
By any other name would smell as sweet;
So Romeo would, were he not Romeo call'd,
Retain that dear perfection which he owes
Without that title. Romeo, doff thy name,
And for that name which is no part of thee
Take all myself.

Another quote regarding names occurs in the Book of Genesis, chapter 2, verses 19–23. (The New English Bible, with the Apocrypha. Oxford University Press, 1970)

So God formed out of the ground all the wild animals and all the birds of heaven. He brought them to the man to see what he would call them, and whatever the man called each living creature, that was its name. Thus the man gave names to all cattle, to the birds of heaven, and to every wild animal; but for the man himself no partner had yet been found. And so the Lord God put the man into a trance, and while he slept, he took one of his ribs and closed the flesh over the place. The Lord God then built up the rib, which he had taken out of the man, into a woman. He brought her to the man, and the man said:

Case 40

> 'Now this, at last—
> bone from my bones,
> flesh from my flesh!—
> this shall be called woman,
> for from man was this taken.'

What exactly happens here? The name Montague carries with it a host of fixed conceptions. Being a Montague, Romeo has to be an enemy of the Capulets because that's the way things are. That was the current state of the feud that had gone on for many years between the Montagues and the Capulets. The key word is "fixed." A name tends to "fix" a person. A name robs one's divinity. A name takes a person out of the realm of no-place and plants that person some-place, thereby fixing that person with a particular personality, a particular set of opinions, a particular narration to their life, et cetera. The real place, which is no-place, is complete and is the place we are in. That is the place we seek to find in zazen. In the myths of Christianity and Judaism, the Western myths of Genesis, we find that the first man, Adam, names everything. All the animals. All the trees. All the flowers, plants, birds, mountains. He fixes everything. He names the first woman. I wonder if this is the Fall, rather than the eating of the fruit! Rather than disobedience! Before Adam named names, Genesis says earlier in chapter 1, verse 27:

> So God created man in his own image; in the image of God he created him; male and female he created them.

Yun-chu

No names! Male and female are OneBody. Names separate. Names fix. Names do not identify. Just the contrary. They confuse. They disassociate. Now of course we live in the world of duality. We live in the world of names. Yet we should know there is a realm of no-name. We must know that the names we use are relative, transitory, shifting, and they all are lies. The truth is that there is no name. No place. No thing. There is! It is! When one is in a lighted room, one doesn't turn on the lights. It would be crazy. The lights are on. Naming turns the lights off.

Poem

Yun-chu

There's an eternity of names
in the warehouse of the universe.

Names for every flower, tree or shrub;
names for every animal, fish or bird;
names for people, babies being born;
names for baptisms, jukais, *confirmations;*
names for chemicals, drugs, diseases, cures;
names for baseball, hockey, basketball, and
  football teams;
names, names, names
names for everything imaginable.

But nowhere do I find the name
of the name that has no name.

Case 41

T'ung-an Tao-p'i

The fortieth ancestor was Zen master T'ung-an Tao-p'i. Once, Yun-chu said, "If you want to acquire such a thing, you must become such a person. Since you are such a person, why be anxious about such a thing?" Hearing this, the master was awakened.

Keizan's Verse
Seeking it oneself with empty hands, you return with empty hands;
In that place where fundamentally nothing is acquired, you really acquire it.

Thoughts

Again we are face-to-face with the Light. The point of this koan is that no matter how hard we look for the Light we cannot find it. Looking itself is the Light. Yet by looking we will not find the Light. As I said in the last case, when we are in darkness, there is no light. All the looking around for the Light will not reveal it. There is no switch that turns on the Light. Light-switching is a delusion we invent. We think somewhere there is a button or switch one can press

T'ung-an Tao-p'i

and bingo! No. In darkness, there is no Light. Light exists within itself. Where then is the Light? Repeatedly Keizan tell us. It is within. The Buddha says, "Look within." Why don't we believe it? Why do we keep looking for light-switches? Buttons? Dimmers? Undimmers? Zazen will help us find that which we have covered over with the obfuscations of centuries. Obfuscations of opinions, habits, prejudices, learning, theories, religions, zen practices, all of which is not the Light. The Light is not something to find. Not something to buy. Nor something to uncover. I believe once we realize this, we will see the Light. And we will see in the dark. Sekito Kisen says, "Light is also darkness. But do not move with it as darkness." Do not see it as darkness. Light is Light.

Poem

T'ung-an Tao-p'i

I dreamt the moon was gone
I rubbed my eyes
rose from my bed
and all was dark.

I flicked the light switch
but there was no light,

I went outside
and searched behind every tree
under every rock
looking for the moon.

Case 41

*I stumbled in the dark
searching, stumbling,
screaming for the moon.*

*I stubbed my toe upon a rock,
and awakened with a start.*

*My eyes blind with light
saw the moon resting safe
within my heart.*

CASE 42

T'ung-an Kuan-chih

The forty-first ancestor was great master T'ung-an the Latter. He studied with the former T'ung-an. He said, "The ancients said, 'What worldly people love, I love not.' I wonder what you love." T'ung-an Tao-p'i said, "I have already been able to be like this." With these words, the master was greatly awakened.

Keizan's Verse
*The light of the Mind-moon and colors of the
    eye-flower are splendid;
Shining forth and blooming beyond time who
    can appreciate them?*

Thoughts

This is a koan about attachment. It is interesting to again compare the translations of Cook and Cleary. Cook uses the word "love" whereas Cleary says, "care for." Cleary says, "I have already gotten to be thus." Cook says, "I have already gotten to be like this."

Case 42

Later on in the commentary, Keizan castigates love as the greatest cause of attachment. Keizan says it is possible to attach to forms as well as formlessness and both are traps. One can even attach to Buddha, Buddhism, Zen, zazen, practice—all are traps.

I don't quite agree with Keizan's use of the word "love." I believe one should love. I believe loving makes all the sense in the world.

But I distinguish between loving which frees and loving which binds. There is a love that makes one want to own the loved one as an object. We want to own our husbands or wives. We want to own our gardens and homes. We want to own our books, our computers. In a sense we do. But if we look deeper, we realize it is impossible to own anything. Jesus said we cannot add a cubit to our height. We cannot add a hair to our head. We cannot add an eyelash. We are complete as we are. How can you add to completeness? We don't have the brains, or the psychological knowledge and technological development, to add a hair. Someday we probably will. But that's another matter.

We should realize that all we have, we have in trust. The song says, "You can't take it with you." We can't even take our bodies with us. We live in a world of dualities. We live in a world of attachments. Attachments to things, persons, feelings, opinions, habits we refuse to relinquish. We hold on to them. We refuse to let them go. The hundred-foot pole is the pole of attachments and we won't let go of it. We hang on for dear life.

T'ung-an Kuan-chih

We want to reshape whatever we touch, whatever we love, into our own image, into our own habit-formations. We want others to be in accord with our own opinions and prejudices. We want that which we love to like that which we like.

It is possible to love one's things, one's husband or wife or lover or children, without attaching to them. To love in a way that frees them to be themselves. It's tricky, but I think it's possible.

In the place of openness—in the place of notknowing—we find true love, true freedom.

Poem

T'ung-an Kuan-chih

to study the way
is to forget the way
and to kick Dogen
in the pants

CASE 43

Liang-shan

The forty-second ancestor was priest Liang-shan. He studied with T'ung-an the Latter and served him. T'ung-an asked him, "What is the business beneath the patch robe?" The master had no answer. T'ung-an said, "Studying the Buddha Way and still not reaching this realm is the most painful thing. Now, you ask me." The master asked, "What is the business beneath the patch robe?" T'ung-an said, "Intimacy." The master was greatly awakened.

Keizan's Verse
The water is clear to the very bottom;
The pearl gleams naturally, without need of cutting and polishing.

Thoughts

This case is a paean to the Unborn. In his *teisho* on this case, Keizan reaches the sublime heights of Paul in his Letter to the Corinthians. Consider the texts. Paul, in I Corinthians, chapter 1, verse 13, says:

Liang-shan

I may speak in tongues of men or of angels, but if I am without love, I am a sounding gong or a clanging cymbal. I may have the gift of prophecy, and know every hidden truth; I may have faith strong enough to move mountains; but if I have no love, I am nothing. I may dole out all I possess, or even give my body to be burnt, but if I have no love, I am none the better.

And now Keizan's words:

Even if you demolish your meditation seat from prolonged sitting and persevere mindless of fatigue, and are a person of lofty and spotless conduct, if you haven't reached this realm, it will be hard for you to escape the prison of the triple world. Even if you possess the four kinds of eloquence and the eight sounds, and your preaching covers everything like mist, your speech rolls like the waves in the sea, your Dharma preaching astounds heaven and earth, and you make flowers rain from the sky and make rocks move. Still, if you have not yet reached this realm, old Yama, Lord of the Dead, will not fear your eloquence. Even if you practice for an exceedingly long time, exterminate thoughts and still your emotions, make your body like a withered tree and your mind like ashes, mind never reacting to external things, and never losing mindfulness when confronting events; and you become liberated while sitting, or die while standing; and you seem to have acquired independence and freedom with regard to life and death, if you have still not reached this realm, all that is valueless in the house of the Buddha ancestors.

Studying the Buddha Way and still not reaching this realm "is a most painful thing." What is this realm? It is the realm of the Unborn. Where is it? It is within. As simple as that. And what is the great matter? It is *being* the Unborn, Buddha-nature, the Holy Spirit, the True Self. That's

Case 43

what it's all about, says Keizan. That's what zazen is all about. It's about eating and drinking, sleeping, walking in the woods, reading Shakespeare, listening to Bach, Beethoven, Charlie Parker, Benny Goodman, and Mozart. It's about the Unborn. How do we reach the Unborn? Bankei tells us very clearly. Turn to it. It's as simple as the first steps of meditation—counting one's breath: one, two, three, four . . . oops! One, two, three, four . . . oops! One two, three, four . . . oops! Back to one.

Poem

Liang-shan

The realm beyond the realm
beyond the realm
is never there.

The realm beyond the realm
beyond the realm
is always here.

Like biting a jalapeño.

CASE 44

Ta-yang

The forty-third ancestor was great master Ta-yang. Once, he asked Priest Liang-shan, "What is the formless site of enlightenment?" Liang-shan pointed to a picture of the Bodhisattva Kuan-yin and said, "This was painted by the scholar Wu." The master was about to speak when Liang-shan suddenly grabbed him and said, "This is what has form; what is it that has no form?" With these words, the master comprehended.

Keizan's Verse
The mind mirror hangs high and reflects everything clearly;
The vermilion boat is so beautiful that no painting can do it justice.

Thoughts

More on Buddha-nature, the Unborn, the Light. What is it that babies see before they can see? Immediately after birth they stare intently. Deeply. Their eyes are wide open. They cannot see. Yet they see. What do they see? Do they see the

Case 44

bodhisattvas and the angels? Do they see the Wooden Man and the Stone Woman? Do they see the Light? The Unborn? Is there recognition in their eyes? Is it all amazement? Is it all "Ahhhhhhhhh!"

One evening I saw a TV program about diseases of the mind. One disease was characterized by the inability to remember what one sees. Even looking into a mirror, one does not recognize oneself. One doesn't know who is looking back. What a painful, terrible thing. One has to relearn how to see. What became clear in this film is that seeing does not involve seeing. Seeing involves all that we are, all that we have experienced, from the first gaze of wonder to the present. In the diseased state of mind, of the brain, one does not know what a tree is, or a house, or a cat, or a book. One does not recognize one's wife, or one's children.

Recently, in an article in *The New Yorker*, I read about a person born blind who regained the power of sight in his forties through the miracle of surgery. That person, like the person with the diseased brain, could not see! He didn't know what he was looking at. He did not know what a tree was, or a house; who his children were or his wife. He didn't know what was looking back at him in the mirror. He had to re-learn all these things. In exasperation, he said he saw better when he was blind—when he didn't see.

So what is it one sees when one sees? What is it that sees? What is it that has form? What is no form? We are dealing with a realm beyond our senses. A realm that contains the face we had before we were born. A realm of the

Ta-yang

true self. Of the Unborn. Of the Light. The realm of the singing Wooden Man and the dancing Stone Woman.

Poem

Ta-yang

Entering a blade of grass
I squiggle through
my rockhard mind.

I see the faceless face
I had before I was born.

I see the Stone Woman dance
to the song of the Wooden Man.

Case 45

T'ou-tzu

The forty-fourth ancestor was priest T'ou-tzu. He studied with Ta-yang. Ta-yang had him inspect the story of the nonbuddhist, asking the Buddha, "Aside from speech, aside from silence." After three years, one day Ta-yang asked him, "Do you remember the case? Try to present it." The master was about to speak when Ta-yang put his hand over T'ou-tzu's mouth. The master was thoroughly enlightened.

Keizan's Verse
The outline of a peak so high that birds can hardly cross;
Sword blades and thin ice—who can walk on them?

Thoughts

This koan challenges us to express the inexpressible. Our dilemma is that we are practicing a Way that is inexpressible. We are practicing a Way that has no forms or non-forms. No creeds. No formulas. No answers. The very practices of Zen are hindrances. The practices themselves are not the Way. The challenge is to express the Absolute by means of the Relative. Speech, in this koan, is the Relative; silence is the Absolute. The Heart Sutra tells us form is emptiness; emptiness is form. The Relative is in the Absolute and the Absolute is in the Relative. So we have a Himalayan contradiction.

Earlier, I said practice is not the Way. But now I say, with Dogen, that practice *itself* is the way. The practice of zazen, the counting of the breaths, forgetting and drifting into thought, catching the drift, returning to one, is the Way. The koan *Mu* is the Way. But as soon as we say it, we miss it. One can also say we are divine beings encased in a skinbag of flesh and bones. Yet this body of skin and bones is a temple. How do we express our divinity? If this sounds blasphemous, try to look at it in a new way. If we have the Light within, Buddha-nature, the Unborn, the Holy Spirit, then we are divine! There is divinity within. The Absolute is within this timorous, frail, fragile, corruptible body of ours.

So how do we express this? How do we walk the Way? What words can we use? What nonwords? What actions? What nonactions? If we think zazen is the Way, we're wrong. If we do not think zazen is the Way, we're wrong. How do we get out of this conundrum? It's like a maze. Wherever we turn, we find our way blocked. What is the cause of the blockage? How do we find our way through the labyrinth? It seems all avenues are blocked. But we know in our bones, in every fiber of our beings, that there is an opening, there is a way. That's what koan

Case 45

study is about. That's why we do koan study. A koan is a conundrum. It's a maze. There seems to be no way through the koan. What is the answer to the koan *Mu*? There is no answer. *Mu*, plain and simple. What is the answer to the sound of one hand? There is no sound. One hand cannot make a sound. Yet we know in our bones that it can. How? What's it all about? It seems impossible to find our way through these koans. Yet we work with them inch by inch, breath by breath, until we see an opening.

Poem

T'ou-tzu I

*Use the delusory Pole
as a catapult—
to crash through the
black hole of Doubt
and enter the Dragon Gate
of the Unknown Heart—
where there is no
spoken or unspoken.*

T'ou-tzu II

*To see beyond seeing—
hear beyond hearing—
think beyond thinking—
is to miss the Way.*

Case 46

Fu-jung

The forty-fifth ancestor was Zen master of Mount Fu-jung. He studied with priest T'ou-tzu. He asked T'ou-tzu, "The words of the Buddha ancestors are like ordinary rice and tea, but is there anything else apart from these to help people?" T'ou-tzu replied, "Tell me, does the emperor's mandate in his kingdom depend on the ancient emperors Yao, Shun, Yu, and T'ang?" The master was about to answer when T'ou-tzu struck him in the mouth with his *hossu* and said, "When you gave way to thought, you immediately deserved thirty blows." The master was awakened.

Keizan's Verse

Even without cosmetics, no ugliness shows;
We naturally admire the ornaments of
   lustrous jade bones.

Thoughts

The central theme of the *Denkoroku* is the transmission of the Light. In one way or another, each case opens a different door to the Light. All doors lead to the Light. This case

Case 46

is about the teachings of the buddhas and the ancestors. How should we hold these teachings? How do we hold the sutras? Zen is a way outside the sutras and outside the teachings. Indeed, Zen brazenly proclaims there are no teachings. What then of the words of the Zen ancestors? Are we to disregard them?

The Buddha tells a story of a raft. A man was going on a journey. He came to a river that was impossible to cross on foot. So he built a raft from the straw and reeds and planks of wood he found along the riverside. He then managed to row himself across the river on the raft. Once he got to the other side, he continued his way on foot, leaving the raft behind.

The teachings, the sutras, Zen practice, the words you are hearing or reading right now, are rafts. Rafts that may help you cross the river. Once across, it's crazy to carry the raft on dry land. Drop it, and be on your way. Once we have opened the door and seen the Light, nothing else matters. That's it! We can get on with our lives; drink our wine and eat our pasta. The Way then becomes a way of wine and pasta.

Poem

Fu-jung

The words of the Buddhas
and all the Zen masters
illumine the sky
like brilliant fireworks
and then are gone.

Fu-jung

*To use these words
is like making coffee
with the same grounds
over and over again.*

Case 47

Tan-hsia

The forty-sixth ancestor was Zen master Tan-hsia. He asked Fu-jung, "What is the single phrase that all the sages have transmitted from ancient times?" Fu-jung replied, "If you call it a phrase, you really bury the Ts'ao-tung tradition." With these words, the master was greatly awakened.

Keizan's Verse
The pure wind circles the earth and shakes it time after time,
But who can pluck it up and show it to you?

Thoughts

"What is the single phrase that all the sages have transmitted from ancient times?" This misses the point! There's no phrase. Light is transmitted. Repeatedly we turn to words, teachings, sutras, Zen practice, liturgy, mass, Holy Communion. The point of Holy Communion is to become one with Christ. So that Christ feels Christ within. The point of Zen practice is to reach the Light. There is no way to unlock the lock of the door to the Light. There is no door, much less a lock to unlock.

Poem

Tan-hsia

4 A.M.
dawn zazen
nameless stream
rushes down the mountain
pours into the Stonykill

chorus of cicadas,
crickets
frogs
smell of incense
flicker of candle
silent breathing
silence

or

breakfast
a cup of coffee
a slice of lemon-blueberry cake
ahh

or

CASE 48

Chen-hsieh

The forty-seventh ancestor was Zen master Chen-hsieh. He studied with Tan-hsia. Tan-hsia asked him, "What is the Self prior to the empty eon?" The master started to speak and Tan-hsia said, "You're noisy; go away for a while." One day, Chen-hsieh climbed Po-yu Peak and was suddenly awakened.

Keizan's Verse
*The icy spring of the valley stream—no one peeks into it.
It does not allow travelers to penetrate its depth.*

Thoughts

A famous koan all of us need to work through is "What is the face I had before I was born?" This is another way of asking, What is my True Self? What is the Light? The Unborn Buddha Mind? The Holy Spirit? In koan study we must present this face. How to present it? All words are noisy. All actions are noisy. Yet we must make a presentation to pass the koan. Present the Face. Present the Light. Present the Holy Spirit.

It is interesting that these statements use the word "present," which has the identical spelling for the word "present," to be here. How do we present the present? How is the present presented? Present the present? Present presented.

Poem

Chen-hsieh I
(a noisy poem)

the face I had
before I was born
is the face I had
before I was born
is the face I had
before I was born
before I was the face
I had before I was born
before I was born
before the face
I had before I was born
I had the face I had
before I was born

Chen-hsieh II

the face I had before I was born
is the face I had before I was born

CASE 49

T'ien-t'ung Tsung-chueh

The forty-eighth ancestor was Zen master T'ien-t'ung Tsung-chueh. He was Chen-hsieh's attendant for a long time. One day, Chen-hsieh asked him, "How do you see it these days?"

The master said, "Suppose I say that I am like this."

Chen-hsieh said, "That's not enough; say some more."

The master replied, "Why isn't it enough?"

Chen-hsieh answered, "I didn't say it was not enough, but you aren't familiar with that which is beyond."

The master said, "I expressed that which is beyond."

Chen-hsieh then asked, "What is that which is beyond?"

The master replied, "Even supposing that I can express that which is beyond, I cannot put it into words for you, master."

Chen-hsieh said, "You can't really express it."

The master said, "I beg you to say it."

Tien-t'ung Tsung-chueh

Chen-hsieh answered, "Ask me, and I'll say it."

The master asked, "What is that which is beyond?"

Chen-hsieh replied, "Suppose I say that I am not like this." The master was awakened when he heard this, and Chen-hsieh gave his approval.

Keizan's Verse
It is like trying to drive a wedge between two planks;
You can't drive in the wedge or pry them apart.

Thoughts

This koan asks, What is that which is beyond? Is there such a thing as beyond? If there is OneBody, can there be anything beyond it? OneBody encompasses everything including beyond. The heavens, the earth, the seas, and all life within the heavens, the earth, the seas. All the trees, rivers, mountains, the angels, the bodhisattvas, gods, goddesses, demons, the dreams, the aspirations, you and me.

To think of anything beyond is to separate OneBody. It can't be done. Keizan's verse says we can't drive in a wedge or pry them apart. Because there is no other. There is no separation.

Case 49

Separation implies there are no consequences to our acts. But we know that whatever we do, say, think, feel, has a consequence. Whenever we say "this," "that" happens. That's the way it is. Everything we do affects the universe. The farthest star feels my indifference.

Poem

T'ien-t'ung Tsung-chueh

Sifting through scraps of space
I came upon a speck of star
I opened its door and looked inside
and there I found my heart.

CASE 50

Hsueh-tou

The forty-ninth ancestor was Zen master Hsueh-tou. T'ien-t'ung, one day entered the hall and said, "The World-Honored One spoke with a hidden meaning, but it was not concealed to Mahakashyapa." When the master heard this, he was suddenly awakened to its profound meaning. Standing there in the ranks with the others, his tears fell. He unconsciously burst out, "Why haven't I heard this before?" T'ien-t'ung finished his talk and summoned the master. He asked, "Why were you weeping?" The master replied, "The World-Honored One spoke with a hidden meaning, but it was not concealed to Mahakashyapa." T'ien-t'ung gave his approval, saying, "You must be the one that Yun-chu predicted."

Keizan's Verse
It is called the indestructible hidden body;
That body is empty and bright.

Case 50

Thoughts

There is a paradox in this case. "The World-Honored One spoke with a hidden meaning, but it was not concealed to Mahakashyapa." The paradox lies in the fact that when Buddha spoke, he spoke openly and clearly. There were no hidden meanings. In the *Mahaparinibbana Sutta*, (16.2.25), which is an account of the Buddha's last days, he clearly says:

> I have taught the Dhamma, Ananda, making no "inner" and "outer": the Tathagata has no "teacher's fist" in respect of doctrines.

The Buddha has nothing to hide. No "secret" teachings held in a clenched fist. Everything is out in the open.

So why does this case speak of a hidden meaning? What is the hidden meaning? What is hidden is our understanding. When we don't understand the thing, it is hidden from us. What is it that is hidden from us? Keizan quotes the ancients who say, "Learning the Way is like making fire by rubbing two sticks together. Do not stop for a second when you see smoke." It will always be hidden if we stop when we see smoke. We must keep rubbing rubbing rubbing the sticks until we burst into flame. Then all is revealed. Then nothing is hidden. Then we see there is no darkness in light. Then we see that darkness is also light.

Poem

Hsueh-tou

The heart that
is not
is the heart
that is.

The heart that is
is the heart
that is not.

Case 51

T'ien-t'ung Ju-ching

The fiftieth ancestor was priest T'ien-t'ung Ju-ching. He studied with Hsueh-tou. Hsueh-tou asked him, "Disciple Ju-ching, how can something that has never been soiled be cleaned?" The master spent more than a year on this question. Suddenly, he was awakened, and said, "I have hit upon that which is not soiled."

Keizan's Verse
The wind of the Way, circulating everywhere,
    is harder than diamond;
The whole earth is supported by it.

Thoughts

We now arrive at the great Ju-ching, the Zen master who Dogen Zenji found just as he was about to leave China in despair at not having found a true teacher. What would Zen be today if Dogen had not found Ju-ching? Once Dogen found Ju-ching he knew this was the master: Ju-ching.

What is striking about Ju-ching for me is his uncompromising rejection of all pomp and circumstance. Throughout his entire life he remained a simple monk, never wearing the grand robes and *rakusus* of different

T'ien-t'ung Ju-ching

colors appropriate to his office. His robe was always a simple black. A monk among monks.

What is also equally remarkable about Ju-ching is his openness. There were several Taoist priests who applied to study with him at his monastery. He welcomed them, and did not require that they convert to Buddhism to remain in the monastery or to study with him. So we have the first interfaith Zen community. Here is the first statement that it is not necessary to be a Buddhist to practice Zen.

Turning to our case: By now we know that which has never been defiled. Or do we? Is it possible to defile the Unborn, the Holy Spirit, Buddha-nature? The last of the Ten Great precepts is "I vow not to speak ill of the Three Treasures." Is speaking ill of the Three Treasures a defilement? A soiling? Can we clean something that is not dirty and was never soiled? What is the process of purification? In an earlier poem, I indicate this process is "One, two, three, four . . . oops! One, two, three, four . . . oops! One, two, three, four . . . oops!" How does this process purify? And what is purified?

Poem

T'ien-t'ung Ju-ching

The moon spears all creation
with its cool, penetrating light.

Each blade of grass,
each busy ant,
each leaf,
each solitary heart,
receives the melancholy stigmata.

CASE 52

Eihei Dogen

The fifty-first ancestor was priest Eihei Dogen. He studied with priest T'ien-t'ung Ju-ching. Once, during late night zazen, Ju-ching told the monks, "Studying Zen is the dropping off of body and mind." Hearing this, the master was suddenly greatly awakened. He went at once to the abbot's room and burned incense. Ju-ching asked him, "Why are you burning incense?" The master answered, "Body and mind have dropped off." Ju-ching said, "Body and mind have dropped off, the dropped-off body and mind." The master said, "This is a temporary ability, you must not approve me without reason." Ju-ching replied, "I am not approving you without reason." The master asked, "Why are you not approving me without reason?" Ju-ching said, "You have dropped off body and mind." The master bowed. Ju-ching said, "You have dropped off dropping off."

Then Ju-ching's attendant, Huang-p'ing of Fu-chou, said, "It is no small thing for a foreigner to experience this realm." Ju-ching said, "How many here have gotten it? Liberated, he is mild and peaceful, and the thunder roars."

Keizan's Verse
That bright and shiny realm has neither inside nor outside;
How can there be any body and mind to drop off?

Thoughts

It is just about impossible to appreciate the genius of Dogen. Dogen was a child prodigy comparable to Wolfgang Amadeus Mozart. At the age of six, Dogen, born in Japan, had already mastered classical Chinese and presented a volume of poems, written in Chinese, to his uncle. By the age of seventeen, he had read the entire Buddhist canon. He thoroughly studied the way of Taoism, Shingon, Tendai, and Rinzai Zen. He received transmission in Rinzai Zen. Later, in China, he received transmission from Ju-ching in the Soto Zen lineage while in his twenties! Truly, a remarkable achievement. The Soto lineage, therefore, is imbued with these other traditions. Dogen's writing reflects his vast knowledge and erudition.

At the end of his *teisho* to this koan, Keizan speaks of a punctured cup. He goes a step beyond a metaphor I used earlier of the empty cup. The way to pursue Zen practice is

Case 52

to have a cup punctured with holes. Whatever is placed in the cup immediately pours out. Always empty. Dropping body and mind—this is the punctured cup. When the cup is punctured, there is no inside or outside. There is no cup. There is only the Light. Then, dropping off body and mind is dropped.

Poem

Eihei Dogen

drop the hole in the bucket
dear Liza dear Liza

drop the wooden man
drop the stone woman

drop the unseeing eyes
drop the unhearing ears

drop body drop mind
drop no-body drop no-mind

drop dropping

Case 53

Koun Ejo

The fifty-second ancestor was priest Koun Ejo. He studied with priest Dogen. Once, while asking for instruction, he heard the expression "a single hair pierces many holes," and was awakened. That evening, he made his bows to Dogen and asked, "Irrespective of the single hair, what are the many holes?" Dogen smiled and said, "Completely pierced." The master bowed.

Keizan's Verse
Space, from the beginning, has not admitted
 even a needle;
Vast, nonreliant, it is beyond all discussion.
Do not say that a hair passes through the
 many holes;
Empty and spotless, it is unmarked by any scars.

Thoughts

At last we come to the final case of the *Denkoroku*. Keizan again reaches great heights of eloquence in describing the Light. In the final paragraphs he writes:

Case 53

Even though the myriad things are extinguished, there remains something that is not extinguished. Even though everything is gone, there is something that is not exhausted. It turns out to be as expected, naturally. Utterly empty, it is marvelously bright by nature. Therefore, it is said to be pure and naked, empty and spotless, obvious, bright, and shining. There is not a hair of doubt, not a whisper of false thought. It is brighter than a billion suns and moons. You cannot say it is white, you cannot say it is red. It is like waking from a dream. It is simply vivid alertness within yourself, so we call it "vivid alertness." Calling it "alertness" means just that you are very awake. Calling it "bright" means just that it is very bright. You do not have to say that it has neither inside nor outside, nor is there any need to say that it extends into the past and extends into the present. Therefore, do not say that "a single hair pierces many holes." What complete piercing can there be?

This hymn of Light is the conclusion of the Denkoroku.

What are the many holes? Can there be holes in Light? Can there be holes in emptiness? What is punctured? What is the single hair? Finally, what is the Light?

Poem

Koun Ejo

*When all is gone
something still is left—
a something that is nothing
a nothing that is something.*

*It strides
and lights
the universe.*

*Clear—open—complete
it warms the caverns of the heart.*

Soto Zen Lineage Chart

The Indian Ancestors

Shambhala	Zen Light	Cook
Buddha Shakyamuni	Shakyamuni Buddha	Sakyamuni
Mahakashyapa	Mahakashyapa	Mahakasyapa
Ananda	Ananda	Ananda
Shanavasin	Shanavasin	Sanavasa
Upagupta	Upagupta	Upagupta
Dhitika	Dhitika	Dhrtaka
Mishaka	Mishaka	Micchaka
Vasumitra	Vasumitra	Vasumitra
Buddhanandi	Buddhanandi	Buddhanandi
Buddhamitra	Buddhamitra	Buddhamitra
Parshva	Parshva	Parsva
Punyayasha	Punayayasha	Punyayasas
Anabodhi	Anabodhi	Asvaghosa
Kapimala	Kapimala	Kapimala
Nagarjuna	Nagarjuna	Nagarjuna
Kanadeva	Kanadeva	Kanadeva
Rahulabhadra	Rahulabhadra	Rahulata
Samghanandi	Samghanandi	Sanghanandi
Samghayathata	Samghayathata	Gayasata
Kumaralata	Kumaralata	Kumarata
Shayata	Shayata	Jayata
Vasubandhu	Vasubandhu	Vasubandhu
Manorata	Manorata	Manorhita
Haklenayasha	Haklenayasha	Haklenayasas
Simhabodhi	Simhabodhi	Aryasimha
Bashashita	Bashashita	Basiasita
Punyamitra	Punyamitra	Punyamitra
Prajñadhara	Prajñadhara	Prajñatara
Bodhidharma	Bodhidharma	Bodhidharma

Cleary	Zen Community NY
Shakyamuni Buddha	Shakyamuni
Kasyapa	Makakasho
Ananda	Ananda
Shanavasa	Shonawashu
Upagupta	Ubakikuta
Dhrtaka	Daitaka
Micchaka	Mishaka
Vasumitra	Bashumitsu
Buddhanandi	Butsudanandai
Punyamitra	Fudamitta
Parshva	Barishiba
Punyayashas	Anabotei
Ashvaghosa	Funayasha
Kapimala	Kabimora
Nagarjuna	Nagyaharajuna
Kanadeva	Kanadaiba
Rahulata	Ragorata
Sanghanandi	Sogyanandai
Jayashata	Kayashata
Kumarata	Kumorata
Jayata	Shayata
Vasubandhu	Bashubanzu
Manora	Manura
Haklena	Kakurokuna
Sinha	Shishibodai
Vashashita	Bashashita
Punyamitra	Funyomitta
Prajnatara	Hannyatara
Bodhidharma	Bodaidaruma

Soto Zen Lineage Chart (continued)

Chinese Ancestors

Shambhala	Zen Light	Cook
Hui-k'o	Hui-k'o	T'ai-tsu Hui-k'o
Seng-ts'an	Seng-ts'an	Chien-chih Seng-ts'an
Tao-hsin	Tao-hsin	T-ai Tao-hsin
Hung-jen	Hung-jen	Ta-man Hung-jen
Hui-neng	Hui-neng	Ta-chien Hui-neng
Ch'ing-yüan	Ch'ing-yüan	Ch'ing-yüan Hsing-ssu
Shih-t'ou	Shih-t'ou	Shih-t'ou Hsi-ch'ien
Yüeh-shan	Yüeh-shan	Yao-shan Wei-yen
Yün-yen	Yün-yen	Yün-yen T'an-sheng
Tung-shan	Tung-shan	Tung-shan Liang-chieh
Yun-chu	Yun-chu	Yun-chu Tao-ying
—	T'ung-an Tao-p'i	T'ung-an Tao-p'i
—	T'ung-an Kuan-chih	T'ung-an Kuan-chih
Ling-shan	Liang-shan	Liang-shan Yüan-kuan
—	Ta-yang	Ta-yang Ching-hsüan
—	T'ou-tzu	T'ou-tzu I-ch'ing
—	Fu-jung	Fu-jung Tao-k'ai
Tan-hsia	Tan-hsia	Tan-hsia Tzu-ch'un
Chen-hsieh	Chen-hsieh	Chen-hsieh Ch'ing-liao
—	T'ien-t'ung Tsung-chueh	T'ien-t'ung Tsung-chüeh
—	Hsueh-tou	Hsüeh-tou Chih-chien
T'ien-t'ung Ju-ching	T'ien-t'ung Ju-ching	T'ien-t'ung Ju-ching
Dogen Zenji	Eihei Dogen	Eihei Dogen
—	Koun Ejo	Koun Ejo

Cleary	Zen Community NY
Huike (Shenguang)	Taiso Eka
Sengcan	Kanchi Sosan
Daoxin	Daii Doshin
Hongren	Daiman Konin
Huineng	Daikan Eno
Qingyuan	Seigen Gyoshi
Shitou	Sekito Kisen
Yaoshan	Yukusan Igen
Yunyan	Ungan Donjo
Dongshan	Tozan Ryokai
Yunju	Ungo Doyo
Daopi	Doan Dohi
Tongan	Doan Kanshi
Liangshan	Ryozan Enkan
Dayang	Taiyo Kyogen
Touzi	Toshi Gisei
Daokai	Fuyo Dokai
Danxia	Tanka Shijun
Wukong	Choro Seiryo
Zongjue	Tendo Sokaku
Zhijian	Setcho Chikan
Rujing	Tendo Nyojo
Dogen	Eihei Dogen
Ejo	Koun Ejo

About the Chart

In an attempt to clarify the lineage of the Zen ancestors discussed in *Zen Light,* I have assembled the above chart. Unfortunately, there is no set pattern of spelling the names of these ancestors. We especially get into massive confusion with the Chinese Ch'an masters, beginning with Hui-k'o. So, I thought it may make it easier for the reader to figure out who's who by listing the following versions of the names of the ancestors.

In the first column we have the lineage according to *The Shambhala Dictionary of Buddhism and Zen.* I have basically tried to follow this version of the spelling in *Zen Light.* However, I have added the remaining ancestors: T'ung-an Tao-p'i, T'ung-an Kuan-chih, Ta-yang, T'ou-tzu, Fu-jung, T'ien-tung Tsung-chueh, Hsueh-tou, and Koun Ejo.

The second column lists the ancestors I use in *Zen Light,* based on the Shambhala version spellings.

The third column lists the ancestors according to Cook.

The fourth column lists the ancestors according to Cleary.

The fifth column lists the Japanese version of the ancestors' names, as chanted in the Zen Community of New York, the Dragon Gate, and White Cliff Sangas.

For years I smiled at this lineage, knowing that many of the names are fictitious. Some of the masters represented

About the Chart

probably never existed. For instance, there is great doubt as to the historical reality of Bodhidharma, one of the most important ancestors. Then there are others of whom there is no proven historical record. So, if we know this, why do we venerate these ancestors? Why do we reverently, in *gassho* always, chant these ancestors' names daily in our monasteries and Zen communities?

The answer came to me one evening in the prison where I teach Zen. Three of the inmates had studied for two years in order to receive the precepts, or *Jukai*. Part of the study and prepartion is for each student to make a personal list of the ancestors, on a beautiful large parchment chart, known as *Kechimyaku*. Then I take each of the charts, affix a special seal, known as the Three Treasures Seal, upon the names of Shakyamuni, Bodhidharma, Huineng, and Dogen Zenji. Finally, I add the new *dharma* name (which I create for him or her) of the student on the last line of the chart.

We set aside one evening for completing the lineage charts by the *Jukai* students. That evening, the three *Jukai* students sat on chairs in front of tables, so that they could hand-letter their lineage charts. Two senior students from the White Cliff Sangha, of New Paltz, New York, came with me, and assisted the *Jukai* students. It was wonderful. On one side of the room the usual group did zazen. On the other side the three students with their two White Cliff colleagues were working on their lineage charts.

At the end of the session, one of the *Jukai* students brought his chart to me. He wanted me to see it, for he was very proud of the work he had done. He showed me the

About the Chart

line where *his* name would go.

And then I got it! I felt that *he* felt connected! That line, where his name was to be lettered by me, was his direct *connection* to the lineage, going through all of the venerated ancestors to Shakyamuni himself! He counted! He was *connected!* The connection established his reality, and made him personally responsible—to Shakyamuni, Bodhidharma, Hui-neng, Dogen Zenji—to *all* of the ancestors, fictitious or not—for representing the Dharma. It was a very moving moment for me.

And so, I bow to the lineage.